CORE SKILLS

W9-COY-600

Social Studies

ISBN-13: 978-1-4190-3426-8

Steck-Vaughn is a trademark of Harcourt Achieve Inc.

The paper used in this book comes from sustainable resources.

Printed in the United States of America.
6 7 8   0868   14 13
4500408934

Steck Vaughn™

A Harcourt Achieve Imprint

www.HarcourtSchoolSupply.com

Contents

Introduction

Social studies focuses on developing knowledge and skill in history, geography, culture, economics, civics, and government. It also focuses on people and their interaction with each other and the world in which they live. *Core Skills: Social Studies* addresses these areas of study and correlates with national social studies curriculum. With this book, students can:

- gain a better understanding of their country and its regions
- practice map and geography skills
- work with charts and other graphic devices

The book features 15 chapter lessons on a variety of social studies topics. It also includes:

- interactive questions about the text or pictures
- chapter checkups
- unit skill builders to enhance social studies skills
- unit tests for each unit

CHAPTER 1 — A Large and Varied Land

The flag of the United States has one star for each state. How many stars are there?

Where is the United States? What does it look like? How hot or cold is it? These are questions about the **geography** of the United States. Geography is the study of Earth and how we live on it.

Where Is the United States?

The United States is on the **continent** of North America. A continent is a large body of land. The map on page 5 shows North America and the countries that are part of it.

➤ **Find the United States on the map on page 5. Write U.S. next to the United States. _U.S._ is the abbreviation for _United States._**

Look at the map again. The United States looks like a puzzle with many pieces. These pieces are called **states**. There are 50 states. **United** means "together." The name of this country, the United States, means 50 states together.

Forty-eight states are in the part of the country that lies between Canada and Mexico. Each state touches at least one other state. Look at the map key. The dotted lines you see on the map stand for **borders**. Borders separate the states.

➤ **Look at the compass rose on the map on page 5. The letters N, S, E, and W stand for the four cardinal directions. They are North, South, East, and West. Put a ✔ on the country that borders the United States on the south.**

Two states do not touch any other state. They are Alaska and Hawaii. Hawaii is about 2,400 miles away in the Pacific Ocean.

➤ **Find Alaska on the map. What direction is Alaska from Mexico? Write your answer here.**

NW

Some people live in a snowy region.

Regions of the United States

The United States is a very large country. In fact, it's the fourth-largest country in the world. This nation stretches 2,807 miles from the East Coast to the West Coast. And then there are Alaska and Hawaii, too! How can you study something so big?

One way to study this big nation is to divide it into areas called **regions**. The United States can be divided into six different regions:

- Northeast Region
- Southeast Region
- North Central Region
- Rocky Mountain Region
- Southwest Region
- Pacific Region

➤ **Look at the region map on page 7. Find your state. Put a star on it.**

What region is your state in? Write your answer here.

North Central Region

Each region has something special about it. Some regions have lots of mountains, and some are very flat. Some regions get lots of rain, and some are very dry. Some regions are warm most of the year. Some regions get very cold in winter.

The regions of the United States can also be alike. Children in every region go to school. People watch many of the same television shows. They eat many of the same foods. And they do many of the same jobs.

➤ **Look at the map on page 7. Find the region where you live. Color your region. Then choose five colors and shade the remaining five regions on the region map.**

➤ **What do you think is one thing that makes your region special? Tell why. Write your answer here.**

Elkhart, Indiana is special because it's where my loved ones and I live

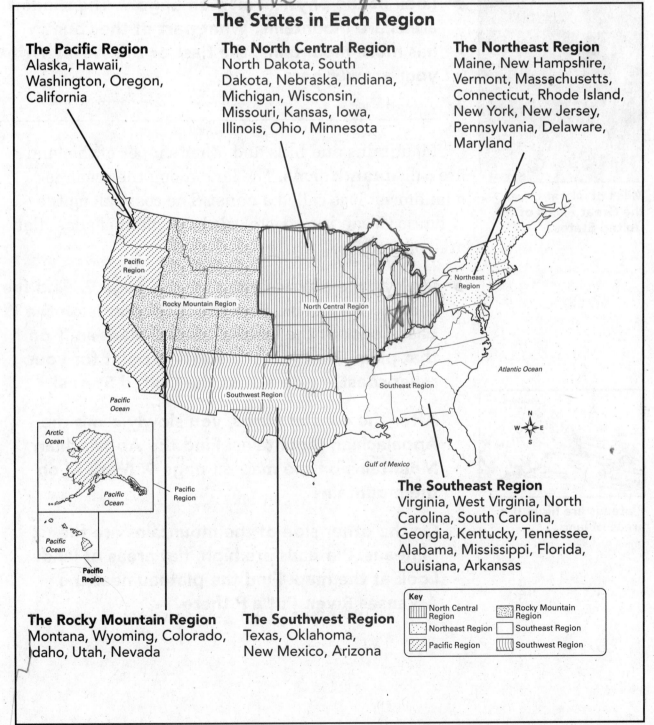

The States in Each Region

The Pacific Region
Alaska, Hawaii, Washington, Oregon, California

The North Central Region
North Dakota, South Dakota, Nebraska, Indiana, Michigan, Wisconsin, Missouri, Kansas, Iowa, Illinois, Ohio, Minnesota

The Northeast Region
Maine, New Hampshire, Vermont, Massachusetts, Connecticut, Rhode Island, New York, New Jersey, Pennsylvania, Delaware, Maryland

The Rocky Mountain Region
Montana, Wyoming, Colorado, Idaho, Utah, Nevada

The Southwest Region
Texas, Oklahoma, New Mexico, Arizona

The Southeast Region
Virginia, West Virginia, North Carolina, South Carolina, Georgia, Kentucky, Tennessee, Alabama, Mississippi, Florida, Louisiana, Arkansas

Key
North Central Region	Rocky Mountain Region
Northeast Region	Southeast Region
Pacific Region	Southwest Region

Miles of wheat cover the Great Plains of the United States.

The Land of the United States

In some ways the land of the United States is like a giant roller coaster. A **physical map** shows where the land is high and where it is low. It can also show the shapes and names of rivers, lakes, deserts, plains, and mountains.

➤ **Look at the physical map on page 9. The shaded areas are mountains. What part of the country has more mountains, the East or the West? Write your answer here.**

West

Mountains and hills and other shapes of the land are called **landforms**. The land along the ocean is a landform. It is called a **coast**. The coast along the Atlantic Ocean is a coastal **plain**. A plain is a low, flat area of land.

➤ **Look at the physical map key on page 9. Find the shading for plains. Find the plain that is on the East Coast of the United States. Mark an <u>X</u> on that plain. That <u>X</u> is the starting point for your roller-coaster ride across the United States!**

After the coastal plains, you slowly climb the Appalachian Mountains. Find the Appalachian Mountains on the map on page 9. Mark <u>M</u> on the mountains.

On the other side of the mountains are the <u>plateaus</u>. Plateaus are high, flat areas of land. Look at the map. Find the plateau near the Arkansas River. Put a <u>P</u> there.

Plateaus are high, flat areas of land.

The roller coaster is zooming across the flat Great Plains. Get ready to climb the Rocky Mountains. They are some of the tallest mountains in the United States!

▶ **Mark another <u>M</u> on the Rocky Mountains.**

Next, you speed down the mountains and across a plateau. After the plateau, you climb more mountains until . . . splash! You're in the ocean!

▶ **Write the name of the ocean here.**

Pacific Ocean

Some regions are very hot and dry.

Climates of the United States

"Wow, it's hot today." "What a storm we had last night!" When you say things like these, you're talking about the **weather**. Weather is made up of several things. Two of these are **temperature** and **moisture**.

Temperature is how hot or cold the air is. Moisture is how wet the air is. The air is very wet when it rains or snows. Weather changes. Today it might rain. Tomorrow it may be hot and dry.

▶ **What two things are part of the weather? Write your answer here.**

temperature and moisture

If you say, "The summers are always very hot where I live," you're talking about the **climate**. The climate is the kind of weather an area has year after year.

You can find out what the weather will be like each day by listening to a weather report. But if you want to find out what the weather will be like all year, you look at a **climate map**. A climate map shows the climate in different areas. Within each area the climate is very much the same.

▶ **The United States has many climates. Look at the climate map key on page 11. Circle the part of the country that usually has cool summers and mild winters and is often wet.**

What kind of summers does Alaska have? Write your answer here.

Wet cool and Dry
Wet

What kind of winters does Puerto Rico have?
Write your answer here.

Ho mild or warm winters

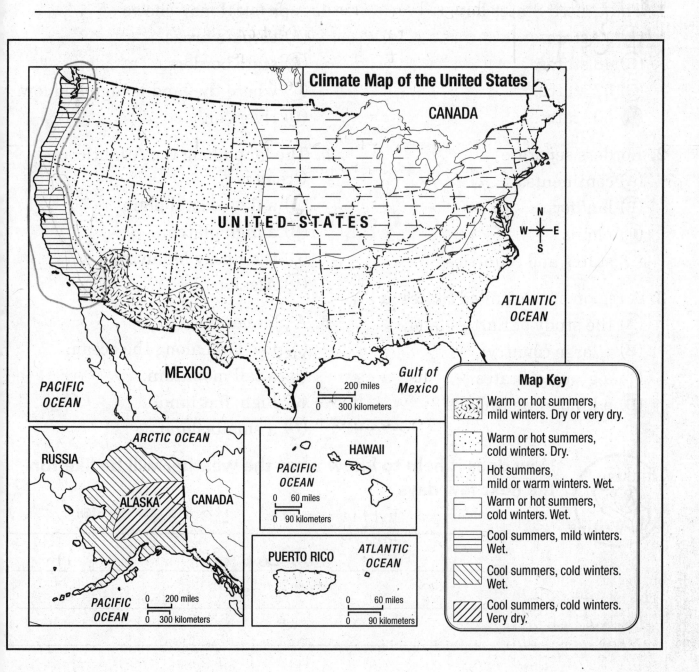

Climate Map of the United States

CANADA

UNITED STATES

N
W · E
S

ATLANTIC OCEAN

MEXICO

PACIFIC OCEAN

Gulf of Mexico

0 200 miles
0 300 kilometers

Map Key

Warm or hot summers, mild winters. Dry or very dry.

Warm or hot summers, cold winters. Dry.

Hot summers, mild or warm winters. Wet.

Warm or hot summers, cold winters. Wet.

Cool summers, mild winters. Wet.

Cool summers, cold winters. Wet.

Cool summers, cold winters. Very dry.

RUSSIA

ARCTIC OCEAN

ALASKA CANADA

PACIFIC OCEAN

0 200 miles
0 300 kilometers

HAWAII

PACIFIC OCEAN

0 60 miles
0 90 kilometers

PUERTO RICO

ATLANTIC OCEAN

0 60 miles
0 90 kilometers

Chapter Checkup ✔

▶ **Darken the circle by the answer that best completes each sentence.**

1. The United States has
   - Ⓐ 13 states.
   - Ⓑ 48 states.
   - Ⓒ 52 states.
   - Ⓓ 50 states.

2. Borders separate
   - Ⓐ continents.
   - Ⓑ landforms.
   - Ⓒ plains.
   - Ⓓ states and countries.

3. A region of the United States is
   - Ⓐ the study of Earth's land.
   - Ⓑ a large country.
   - Ⓒ a group of states.
   - Ⓓ a kind of weather.

4. A physical map shows
   - Ⓐ climate areas.
   - Ⓑ state borders.
   - Ⓒ where the land is high and low.
   - Ⓓ rivers only.

5. The land along the Atlantic Ocean is
   - Ⓐ a flat coastal plain.
   - Ⓑ a high plateau.
   - Ⓒ the Rocky Mountains.
   - Ⓓ Alaska.

6. A plateau is
   - Ⓐ low land along the ocean.
   - Ⓑ a tall mountain.
   - Ⓒ high, flat land.
   - Ⓓ a small island.

Thinking & Writing

How does it help to know what the weather will be like for the next few days?

It helps us to decide What to wear and other things.

_____

_____

_____

_____

CHAPTER 2 · Who Is an American?

Each person who lives in the United States is special in some way. We all live and work together in the United States. We are part of a special group—the American people.

The First Americans

The first people to live in the United States were **American Indians**, or **Native Americans**. *Native* means "the first people to live in a place." American Indians came from Asia to Alaska thousands of years ago. Over time, they settled all over North and South America.

Some American Indians are skilled at weaving rugs.

The American Indians formed hundreds of different groups. Some groups of American Indians lived in small villages and planted crops such as squash, beans, and corn. Other groups traveled to find food and never stayed in one place for very long.

➤ **Where did American Indians who arrived in Alaska come from? Write your answer here.**

New Americans

The first explorers of North America were Vikings. They sailed from Greenland to North America about 1,000 years ago. They did not stay in North America. People in Europe, Asia, and Africa did not know that the Vikings had explored North America.

About 500 years after the Vikings explored North America, Christopher Columbus sailed west from Europe. He landed on an island between North and South America in 1492. Soon other explorers came from Europe.

Later, families from Europe started moving to North America, too. They began **colonies**. A colony is a group of people ruled by another country. The people living in the colonies had to work hard. These **colonists** built homes, farmed, and started businesses.

Homes in the early colonies looked like these homes. They were made of mud and sticks.

▶ **Look at the picture graph below. Sometimes it is easier to understand numbers if you see them as pictures. This graph uses symbols for numbers. This picture graph shows how the colonies grew. How many colonists were there in 1680? How many were there in 1740, 60 years later? Write your answers here.**

1680: _____   **1740:** _____

NUMBER OF COLONISTS IN THE 13 COLONIES (1680–1740)

1680	♀ ♪
1700	♀ ♀ ♪
1720	♀ ♀ ♀ ♀ ♪
1740	♀ ♀ ♀ ♀ ♀ ♀ ♀ ♀ ♀

Each figure ♀ stands for 100,000 people.

New Americans Meet the First Americans

The colonists had come from farms, towns, and cities in Europe. North America was a wilderness area. The colonists had to learn new skills to live in North America. At first, most American Indians were friendly toward the colonists. American Indians taught the colonists about foods they could grow. From Europe, the colonists brought metal tools, guns, cattle, and horses. The American Indians had never seen such things before.

The Pilgrims were early colonists who learned skills from American Indians.

▶ **How did American Indians help the colonists? Write your answer here.**

_____

_____

_____

American Indians wanted to keep living on the land their people had lived on for hundreds of years. The colonists wanted to explore and use the land. They also wanted to build the kinds of towns and farms they remembered from Europe. American Indians and colonists fought many battles about land. The colonists fought with guns. The American Indians used spears and bows and arrows to fight the battles. Because their weapons were less powerful, many more American Indians died during the battles than colonists.

▶ **Why did the American Indians and the European colonists fight about how to use the land? Write your answer here.**

_____

_____

_____

These immigrants from Europe arrived in New York City about 100 years ago.

More New Americans Arrive

Beginning in the 1600s, some Africans were forced to come to this country. These people were sold to colonists as **slaves**. A slave is a person who is owned by another person. Some colonists used slaves to do the hard work on the farms and in the new towns.

In 1861, Americans fought one another in the Civil War. After the war, slaves became free. New laws said that no person could ever be made a slave in the United States again.

During the 1700s and 1800s, many **immigrants** from Europe came to the United States. Immigrants are people who come from one country to live in another country. They wanted a chance to own land or find good jobs.

Today the largest numbers of immigrants come from Asia and Latin America. Today's immigrants, like immigrants of earlier times, hope to find a better life.

▶ **A bar graph uses bars to stand for numbers. The bar graph below shows the countries that many immigrants came from between 1820 and 1950. Circle the name of the country the most immigrants came from.**

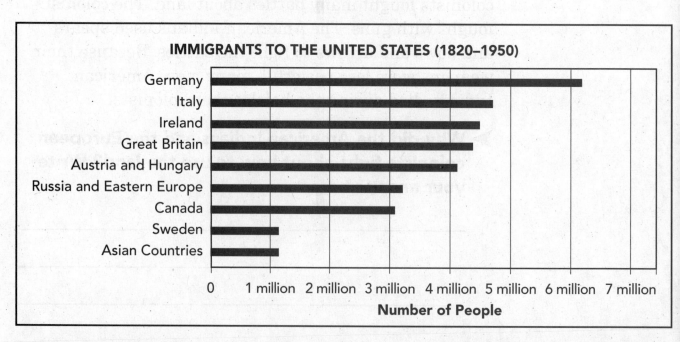

IMMIGRANTS TO THE UNITED STATES (1820–1950)

Germany
Italy
Ireland
Great Britain
Austria and Hungary
Russia and Eastern Europe
Canada
Sweden
Asian Countries

0   1 million   2 million   3 million   4 million   5 million   6 million   7 million

Number of People

Americans Living Together

North Americans have many different backgrounds. Most Americans speak English, but some speak other languages, such as Spanish, Chinese, or Korean. In fact, many words you use each day come from other languages! Did you know that *banana* and *zebra* come from African languages? *Tomato* and *chipmunk* come from American Indian languages!

Although Americans are different in many ways, they are a lot alike. Many Americans enjoy the same foods, such as peanut butter and corn on the cob. Americans do many of the same things, such as play baseball and visit friends. Most importantly, Americans share the same home, the United States of America.

Many different people live in the United States.

Chapter Checkup ✔

➤ Darken the circle by the answer that best completes each sentence.

1. The first Americans were
Ⓐ American Indians.
Ⓑ Puerto Ricans.
Ⓒ African Americans.
Ⓓ Europeans.

2. A colony is
Ⓐ an early American Indian farm.
Ⓑ a place discovered by Columbus.
Ⓒ a land and people ruled by another country.
Ⓓ where African Americans originally came from.

3. From Europe, the early colonists brought metal tools, guns, cattle and
Ⓐ bows and arrows.
Ⓑ horses.
Ⓒ Vikings.
Ⓓ spears.

4. Long ago, some Africans were forced to come to this country as
Ⓐ colonists.
Ⓑ slaves.
Ⓒ settlers.
Ⓓ U.S. citizens.

5. Immigrants are
Ⓐ people who are owned by another person.
Ⓑ people who come from one country to live in another country.
Ⓒ the first Americans.
Ⓓ people looking for jobs.

6. Americans come from
Ⓐ many different countries.
Ⓑ Mexico only.
Ⓒ England only.
Ⓓ Africa only.

Thinking & Writing

Why are most Americans not called Native Americans?

_____

_____

_____

_____

CHAPTER 3 · How Do Americans Live Together?

In the last chapter you read about the many kinds of people who have come to live in the United States. Did you wonder how so many different people can live in one country?

Our Nation's Leaders

It isn't easy for people with different ideas to work and live together. Imagine how hard it would be to drive a car if everyone did what he or she wanted to do. Some people might drive on the right, and some might drive on the left. Some people might even drive on the sidewalks. That's why we have rules to tell drivers where they can drive.

➤ **Write one thing that might happen if there were no rules for people who drive cars. Write your answer here.**

_____

_____

This police officer is talking to students about obeying laws.

Towns, states, and nations need rules, too. Who makes these rules? Groups of people called **governments** do. Rules made by governments are called **laws**. Governments also make sure that the laws are obeyed. We have governments for our towns, our states, and our nation.

A town or city government is called a **local government**. Local governments provide **services** like the police, who work to help and protect us.

➤ **Look at the picture below. Local governments provide this service. Write the reason why this service is important to you.**

_____

_____

Your state government provides services for all the communities in your state. It builds roads between cities. It makes laws about what people can and cannot do in the state.

The government of the United States also makes laws and provides services. For example, it helps maintain highways between states.

Firefighting is a local service. Firefighters must be near homes and businesses.

20

The United States is a **democracy**. That means that the people who live here can **vote** for, or choose, the people in their governments. The people who live in a town vote for the **mayor** of the town. The mayor is the person who leads the town.

The people who live in a state vote for the **governor**. The governor is the person who leads the state. The person who leads the whole country is called the **President**. Almost everyone who is 18 or older can vote to choose the President.

The Capitol building in Washington, D.C.

▶ **Circle the name of the person who leads the United States.**

mayor   governor   President

The President leads the country but does not make the laws. The people who make the country's laws are in **Congress**. Congress has two parts: the **Senate** and the **House of Representatives**.

The people of each state vote for two senators. They also vote for the representatives. The more people there are in a state, the more representatives the state has. Vermont has very few people, so it has only one representative. California has lots of people, so it has 53 representatives.

It is very hard to lead a town, state, or country. It is also hard to make good laws. That is why people have to be very careful when they vote. We must try to pick the best people to be our leaders.

▶ **If you were in Congress, what law would you like to make? Write it here.**

_____

_____

Building a Nation

For hundreds of years, people in the United States have worked hard to build homes and businesses.

Farming has always been important. Many American Indians and colonists were farmers. Today American farms grow food for people in the United States and other countries.

Americans also make a lot of goods. American Indians and early colonists made their own goods by hand. In the 1800s, Americans began making goods in factories.

The way Americans work today is very different from colonial times. Americans have all kinds of jobs. The bar graph on this page shows different job groupings. It also shows how many people work in each job grouping. Today, the **service job** grouping has the largest number of people. People who have service jobs do not *make* anything. People who have service jobs do something to help other people. Service workers might give you a haircut, serve you food, or clean your teeth.

People still make some things, such as quilts, by hand.

➤ **Look at the bar graph. Which job group has about twice as many workers as the construction group?**

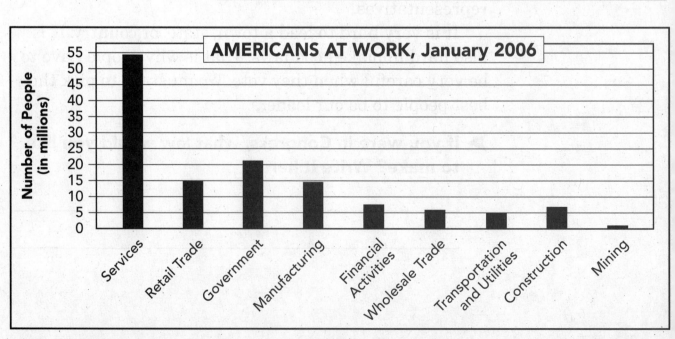

AMERICANS AT WORK, January 2006

(Bar graph showing Number of People (in millions) on the vertical axis, scaled 0 to 55. Job groups on horizontal axis: Services (about 54), Retail Trade (about 15), Government (about 21), Manufacturing (about 14), Financial Activities (about 7), Wholesale Trade (about 6), Transportation and Utilities (about 5), Construction (about 7), Mining (about 1).)

Our Natural Resources

Water and trees are two important resources.

The United States is rich in **natural resources**. Natural resources have helped make our country great. A natural resource is something from nature that we use.

One of the most important resources of the United States is soil. Soil is used to grow crops. Water is another important resource. You probably never realized how important water is. It's so easy to get a glass of water. But if we didn't have much water, we couldn't grow enough food.

➤ **Write two ways you use water.**

_____

_____

Water is useful for other things, too. We use our lakes and rivers to get to places and to move things. Many of our crops and products travel on ships. We also use the power of moving water to make electricity.

When the colonists came from Europe, there were many natural resources. Most people thought the United States had more than enough natural resources. Today we know that some resources will not last forever.

Minerals are one kind of resource that will not last. **Minerals** are materials that are produced by nature, such as iron and coal.

Minerals are usually dug up from the earth. We use iron to make steel. Buildings and cars are made out of steel. We can **recycle** some items made out of minerals, such as steel and aluminum cans. When we recycle, we reuse resources. Reusing resources helps keep us from running out of those resources.

Trees are another great resource. We use them to build homes and furniture. Paper is also made from trees. Before the colonists came, there were forests all over North America. Many forests have been cut down since then. Luckily, trees can be replanted. We have to be careful how many trees we use because trees take a long time to grow.

People can save trees by recycling paper. By recycling paper, we reuse the paper and do not have to cut down as many trees.

➤ **What do we know today about natural resources that the colonists didn't know?**

_____

_____

How Paper Is Recycled

Paper is chopped up into pulp.

Ink is washed out.

Water is drained from pulp.

Paper is dried and rolled.

Chapter Checkup ✓

➤ **Darken the circle by the answer that best completes each sentence.**

1. A group of people who make laws and provide services is called
   - Ⓐ a business.
   - Ⓑ a government.
   - Ⓒ a democracy.
   - Ⓓ a mayor.

2. Rules made by governments are called
   - Ⓐ voters.
   - Ⓑ representatives.
   - Ⓒ laws.
   - Ⓓ democracy.

3. People who vote for their government live in a
   - Ⓐ House of Representatives.
   - Ⓑ democracy.
   - Ⓒ Congress.
   - Ⓓ natural resource.

4. The person who leads a state is called the
   - Ⓐ Senate.
   - Ⓑ Mayor.
   - Ⓒ President.
   - Ⓓ Governor.

5. Soil, water, and forests are all
   - Ⓐ climates.
   - Ⓑ natural resources.
   - Ⓒ services.
   - Ⓓ minerals.

6. People who do something to help other people work in
   - Ⓐ manufacturing.
   - Ⓑ fishing.
   - Ⓒ service jobs.
   - Ⓓ farming.

Why is it important for us to protect our natural resources?

_____

_____

_____

_____

_____

_____

Name _____ Date _____

Unit 1 Skill Builder

Reading a Bar Graph

   During the 1800s and early 1900s, most immigrants came from countries in Europe. Use the bar graph below to find out where some of our country's more recent immigrants have come from.

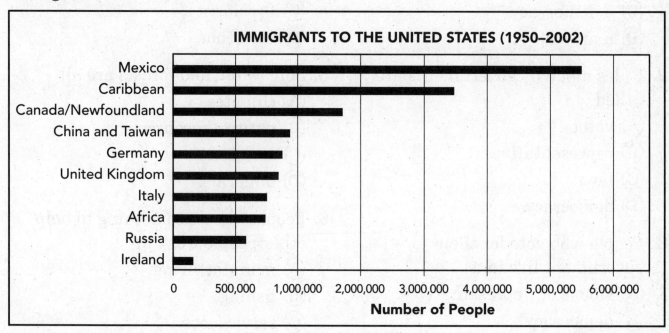

IMMIGRANTS TO THE UNITED STATES (1950–2002)

Mexico
Caribbean
Canada/Newfoundland
China and Taiwan
Germany
United Kingdom
Italy
Africa
Russia
Ireland

0   500,000   1,000,000   2,000,000   3,000,000   4,000,000   5,000,000   6,000,000

Number of People

1. What time period does the bar graph cover?

_____

2. From which country did most immigrants come?

_____

3. About how many immigrants came from Russia?
Circle the correct answer.

500,000   more than 500,000   exactly 1,000,000

4. Compare the bar graph on page 16 to the one on this page. How are they alike? How are they different?

_____

_____

Unit 1 Test

➤ **Darken the circle by the answer that best completes each sentence.**

1. The United States is on the continent of
- (A) North America.
- (B) Canada.
- (C) Mexico.
- (D) South America.

2. Low land along an ocean is called a
- (A) plateau.
- (B) mountain.
- (C) coastal plain.
- (D) climate.

3. Mountains, hills, valleys, and plains are
- (A) reliefs.
- (B) plateaus.
- (C) regions.
- (D) landforms.

4. The first people to live in the United States were
- (A) colonists.
- (B) immigrants.
- (C) American Indians.
- (D) Europeans.

5. A group of people ruled by another country are
- (A) immigrants.
- (B) colonists.
- (C) natives.
- (D) settlers.

6. A government chosen by the people is called
- (A) the Congress.
- (B) the President.
- (C) a democracy.
- (D) a representative.

7. Each of the states has one
- (A) governor.
- (B) Congress.
- (C) senator.
- (D) representative.

8. Natural resources include things like
- (A) representatives and laws.
- (B) governors and Presidents.
- (C) climate and weather.
- (D) soil and water.

How can people living in a democracy change their laws?

_____

_____

_____

CHAPTER 4

Geography of the Northeast Region

You may already know something about the geography of the Northeast Region. You know where this region is in the United States. Its name tells where it is.

States and Cities

There are 11 states in the Northeast Region. Look at the map below. Put your finger on each of the named states.

► **Find the state in the Northeast Region that is the farthest north. Write <u>N</u> on that state.**

Find the state that is the farthest south. Write <u>S</u> on that state.

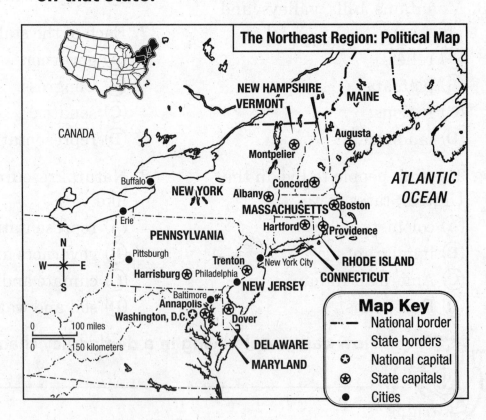

The Northeast Region: Political Map

Map Key

--- ---	National border
---·---	State borders
✪	National capital
⊛	State capitals
●	Cities

A **capital** is a city where a government meets. Washington, D.C., is the capital of our country. It is in the Northeast Region. Washington, D.C., is not like any other city in the United States. It's in a special place called the District of Columbia. We shorten *District of Columbia* to *D.C.*

The Supreme Court

The White House

➤ **Find Washington, D.C., on the map on page 28. It's in the southern part of the region. Use the map key. Find the special star for the national capital. Circle the same star on the map.**

Every state has a capital, too. The state government meets there. There are 11 state capitals in the Northeast Region.

➤ **The map on page 28 has a distance scale. You can use it to find out how far places are from each other. Find Washington, D.C., again on the map. Use the distance scale. About how many miles is Washington from the capital of Pennsylvania? Write your answer here.**

_____

The Land and Water

Pretend that you are planning a bike trip in the Northeast Region. You're going to start on the coast of Maine. Remember, the coast is where the land is next to the ocean. Look at the map and the map key below. Find the plains. Biking is easy on the flat plains along the coast!

There are **highlands** west of the coast. Highlands are hilly areas between flat lands and mountains. Biking will be hard in the highlands.

➤ **Find the shading for highlands in the map key. Draw lines from the key to three highland areas.**

On the map there is shading for the mountains. Circle the Appalachian Mountains. (Remember, *Mtns.* is short for *Mountains*.) Here biking will really be hard!

Bay

You're going to see a lot of water on your trip through the Northeast. Along the coast you will see some large **bays**. A bay is a place where the water is almost surrounded by land. Bays look a little like someone has taken a bite out of the coast.

Bays make safe **harbors** for ships because the water is protected by land. Some big cities like New York City and Boston are on bays. These cities are **ports**. A port is a place where people can load and unload ships.

New York City is on a bay.

▶ **Look at the map on page 30. Find the names of two bays. Write their names here.**

_____

_____

You will cross some big rivers on your trip. The rivers flow into the Atlantic Ocean.

▶ **Look at the map on page 30 again. Trace two of the rivers that flow into the ocean.**

Chapter Checkup ✔

▶ **Darken the circle by the answer that best completes each sentence.**

1. Two of the states in the Northeast Region are
Ⓐ Virginia and Georgia.
Ⓑ New York and Pennsylvania.
Ⓒ Kansas and Nebraska.
Ⓓ California and Hawaii.

2. A capital is
Ⓐ a place where ships are unloaded.
Ⓑ a city where a government meets.
Ⓒ a large river.
Ⓓ near the ocean.

3. Washington, D.C., is
Ⓐ the capital of the United States.
Ⓑ the capital of Maine.
Ⓒ the capital of New York.
Ⓓ the capital of Washington.

4. The land along the coast of the Northeast is
Ⓐ flat.
Ⓑ hilly.
Ⓒ filled with mountains.
Ⓓ a highland.

5. Places that make safe harbors for ships are
Ⓐ capitals.
Ⓑ highlands.
Ⓒ bays.
Ⓓ mountains.

6. In a port, people
Ⓐ live very close to mountains.
Ⓑ load and unload ships.
Ⓒ work on farms.
Ⓓ get on trains.

Thinking & Writing

Pretend that you could live any place in the Northeast. Where would you like to live? Why?

_____

_____

_____

_____

_____

Core Skills Social Studies 4, SV 9781419034268

CHAPTER 5

People of the Northeast Region

The Northeast Region is not just bays, mountains, and big cities. In this chapter you'll learn about the people of the Northeast. Let's begin by visiting the Northeast in the early 1600s, over 400 years ago.

Long Ago: The Pilgrims

Pilgrims traveled on the *Mayflower*.

"Land ho!" a sailor shouted. The people in the little ship looked through the fog. They saw land! These tired people had left England two months before. They had sailed through many storms. At times, they thought their ship, the *Mayflower*, was going to sink. Now, on November 20, 1620, they had finished their trip across the Atlantic Ocean.

We call these people the Pilgrims. They left England because the laws there allowed only one religion. The Pilgrims wanted to practice their own religion.

So the Pilgrims started a colony in North America. There they built their own church and their own school. They called their new town Plymouth, after the city that had been their home in England.

➤ **Why did the Pilgrims leave England? Write your answer here.**

_____

_____

_____

The Pilgrims had many problems that first winter. They had little food, and it was too late in the season to plant crops. It was very cold. Almost half the Pilgrims died that winter. The others thought about going back to England.

► **How did the climate affect the Pilgrims? Write your answer here.**

_____

_____

_____

The Pilgrims were saved by the American Indians who lived near Plymouth. American Indians had lived there for hundreds of years. They knew how to grow and find food. An American Indian named Squanto taught the Pilgrims how to plant corn, catch fish, and even get maple syrup from trees.

American Indians helped the Pilgrims grow crops.

► **Why did the American Indians know more about getting food than the Pilgrims? Write your answer here.**

_____

_____

_____

When spring came, the Pilgrims planted corn and other crops. By the end of the summer, they had a lot of food. They decided to celebrate by having a feast with their new friends.

Before the meal, the Pilgrims gave thanks for the good harvest and for the help the American Indians gave them. They gave thanks for being alive in a new land.

This feast was the first Thanksgiving. Many years later, Thanksgiving became a holiday for everyone in the United States.

Where Do People Live in the Northeast Region?

The Pilgrims were some of the first people to move from their country to North America. But over the years, people came to the Northeast from countries around the world. Today more than 65 million people live in the Northeast.

Most people in the Northeast live in cities. Look at the map of the Northeast on page 28. Find Boston, Massachusetts. Then find Washington, D.C. Imagine a straight line between them. If you rode along that line in a car, you would be in cities most of the time.

➤ **Let's see how far away from each other Boston and Washington, D.C., really are. Use the distance scale on the map on page 28. Measure the distance in miles between these two cities. Write the distance here.**

_____

Many people ride the subway in New York City.

Many people in the Northeast live in **suburbs**. Suburbs are towns or small cities near big cities. Many people who live in suburbs work in the city.

People would have to live very close to their jobs if there was no **transportation**. Transportation is the way people travel to places. People drive on highways or take buses or trains.

➤ **What kinds of transportation do you use in your community? Write your answer here.**

_____

_____

You remember that the Pilgrims began a community called Plymouth. Boston, Massachusetts, is a city near Plymouth. Boston was started by other people soon after the Pilgrims came to Plymouth. Look at the picture of Boston at the top of page 36.

Boston, Massachusetts

Today, Boston is much bigger than Plymouth. One reason Boston is big is because it is by a large bay. Boston is on a river, too. The people who started Boston shipped many goods to England. Boston soon became an important port. Boston is the capital of Massachusetts. Three other port cities in the Northeast are also state capitals.

➤ **Look back at the map on page 28. Can you find the capital cities that are also ports? Write their names here.**

_____ , **Rhode Island**

_____ , **Delaware**

_____ , **Maryland**

One of the most important cities in the region is Baltimore, Maryland. Baltimore is a very old and busy port. Tourists like to visit parts of the old harbor. One area is called Harborplace. People go there to shop and to eat. The National Aquarium is nearby.

Philadelphia, Pennsylvania, is one of the oldest cities in the United States. It was started by William Penn over 300 years ago. Penn's colonists left England so they could practice their own religion.

➤ **How were the colonists of Plymouth and Philadelphia alike? Write your answer here.**

_____

_____

Look at the picture of Independence Hall on this page. It is in Philadelphia. Over 200 years ago, people from all the colonies met there. On July 4, 1776, they decided to start a new country. Many people visit Independence Hall every year.

Working in the Northeast Region

The resources of a region create many jobs. Crops need to be harvested. Trees need to be cut and planted. Food needs to be made. One of the most important resources of the Northeast is the Atlantic Ocean.

➤ **There are 11 states in the Northeast. Look at the map on page 28. Count the states that are next to the ocean. Write the answer here.**

_____

Independence Hall in Philadelphia, Pennsylvania

Can you guess why the Atlantic Ocean is such an important resource? One reason is because it's full of fish!

Early every morning, fishing boats leave the ports of the Northeast. They come back with thousands of fish. The fish are sold to stores all over the Northeast and in other regions.

Most people in the Northeast do not work on fishing boats. Many people have service jobs. Remember that service jobs are jobs that help other people. People who work in stores, offices, and restaurants have service jobs. Firefighters, police officers, and teachers are service workers, too.

Fishing boats in Maine

➤ **How does a firefighter help people?**

_____

_____

Some service jobs in the Northeast help people in other regions of the country. One of these jobs is television news. Television companies have news offices in the Northeast. These offices get reports from around the world. They show news programs that are seen all over the country.

The Pilgrims had to wait many months for a ship to come with news from England. Today's television news programs can show us things as they happen.

Television is one part of a business that is called the communications business. To **communicate** means "to share information." One way people communicate is by talking. Newspapers share news and other information with many people. In fact, any way that news or information goes from one person or place to another is a way of communicating.

Today, many people use computers to communicate. Office workers can use computers to send electronic mail, or E-mail, to other workers who are far away. E-mail is a very quick way of communicating information.

➤ **Write two ways you communicate.**

_____

_____

Manufacturing also provides jobs for many people in the Northeast. People manufacture, or make, all kinds of goods. In the Northeast, most of the goods they make are small, like clocks and books. But there are some companies that make airplanes and other big machines.

Textiles—making thread, yarn, and cloth—has long been an important industry in the region. Thousands of miles of thread are made in factories every day. The thread will be woven into cloth.

Chapter Checkup ✓

➤ **Darken the circle by the answer that best completes each sentence.**

1. The Pilgrims came to the Northeast to
   Ⓐ learn to plant corn.
   Ⓑ be free to practice their religion.
   Ⓒ meet American Indians.
   Ⓓ find New York.

2. Many people in the Northeast live in
   Ⓐ villages.
   Ⓑ colonies.
   Ⓒ bays.
   Ⓓ suburbs.

3. Buses, trains, and cars are types of
   Ⓐ communication.
   Ⓑ transportation.
   Ⓒ manufacturing.
   Ⓓ service jobs.

4. Boston and New York City are
   Ⓐ on the Pacific Ocean.
   Ⓑ state capitals.
   Ⓒ important port cities.
   Ⓓ on the same river.

5. An important resource of the Northeast Region is
   Ⓐ the Atlantic Ocean.
   Ⓑ television news.
   Ⓒ Independence Hall.
   Ⓓ clothing.

6. When you communicate, you
   Ⓐ make goods.
   Ⓑ start colonies.
   Ⓒ use a computer.
   Ⓓ share information.

Thinking & Writing

Why was it important to the Pilgrims for Squanto to teach them how to plant corn and catch fish?

_____

_____

_____

_____

_____

Using a Distance Scale

In this unit you learned about Washington, D.C., the capital of the United States. Suppose you visited Washington. You would probably want to visit some of the city's famous places. Use the map and the distance scale to find out the distances between some of the places you could visit.

1. Find the White House on the map. Then find the Capitol. How many miles is the White House from the Capitol? _____

2. Suppose that after you visited the Capitol, you visited the Library of Congress. About how many kilometers would you travel? _____

3. How many kilometers from each other are the Library of Congress and the Lincoln Memorial? _____

4. The Washington Monument and the Smithsonian Institution look close to each other on the map. What is the real distance in miles between them?

Unit 2 Test

➤ **Darken the circle by the answer that best completes each sentence.**

1. The eastern part of the Northeast Region is along the
   - (A) Pacific Ocean.
   - (B) Rocky Mountains.
   - (C) Atlantic Ocean.
   - (D) Gulf of Mexico.

2. The capital of the United States is
   - (A) New York City.
   - (B) Washington, D.C.
   - (C) Plymouth.
   - (D) Boston, Massachusetts.

3. The hilly areas between flat lands and mountains are called
   - (A) plains.
   - (B) coast.
   - (C) highlands.
   - (D) plateaus.

4. Water that is almost completely surrounded by land is called
   - (A) an ocean.
   - (B) a port.
   - (C) a province.
   - (D) a bay.

5. A city where ships are loaded and unloaded is a
   - (A) port.
   - (B) harbor.
   - (C) capital.
   - (D) suburb.

6. The bays, harbors, and ports in the Northeast are important for
   - (A) communication.
   - (B) service jobs.
   - (C) shipping materials and products.
   - (D) suburbs.

7. The Pilgrims began a community called
   - (A) Boston.
   - (B) Plymouth.
   - (C) Baltimore.
   - (D) Philadelphia.

8. Teachers and firefighters have
   - (A) manufacturing jobs.
   - (B) transportation jobs.
   - (C) service jobs.
   - (D) harbor jobs.

Thinking & Writing

Why do you think many early cities in North America began as port cities?

_____

_____

CHAPTER 6 Geography of the Southeast Region

Welcome to the Southeast Region! It's a land of long, hot summers and mild winters. It's a land of wide plains, rolling hills, and tall mountains.

Where Is the Southeast Region?

There are 12 states in the Southeast Region. Put your finger on each of the labeled states on the map below.

➤ **Write an <u>S</u> on the state that is farthest south.**
Write an <u>N</u> on the state that is farthest north.

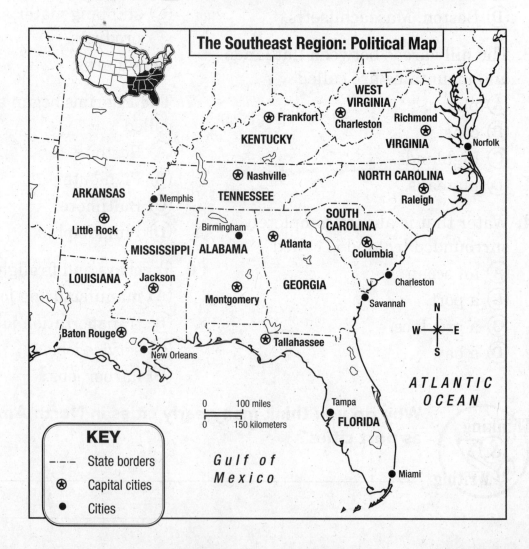

The Southeast Region: Political Map

KEY
- – · – State borders
- ⊛ Capital cities
- • Cities

Core Skills Social Studies 4, SV 9781419034268

Like the states of the Northeast Region, many states in the Southeast Region are next to the Atlantic Ocean.

➤ **Look at the map on page 42. Find the states that are next to the Atlantic Ocean. Circle the names of those states.**

The southern part of the Southeast Region is near the Gulf of Mexico. Like a bay, a **gulf** is a large body of water that joins an ocean. It is partly surrounded by land. Find the Gulf of Mexico on the map.

Certain kinds of bad weather begin over large bodies of water. A **hurricane** is a storm with very strong winds and heavy rain. Some hurricanes start over the Gulf of Mexico and the Atlantic Ocean. Some hit the coast of the Southeast. Hurricanes can kill people. They can destroy buildings and crops.

➤ **Look at this table about hurricanes. A <u>table</u> lists facts so you can compare them easily. Which hurricane caused the most damage? Write the name of the hurricane and the year here.**

_____

Hurricanes of the Southeast			
Name of Hurricane	**Year**	**States Hardest Hit by Hurricane**	**Cost of Damage**
Katrina	2005	Louisiana Alabama Mississippi	$200,000,000,000
Andrew	1992	Florida Louisiana	$7,250,000,000
Hugo	1989	South Carolina	$7,000,000,000
Frederic	1979	Alabama Mississippi	$2,250,000,000
Camille	1969	Mississippi Louisiana Alabama	$1,500,000,000

What Is the Land Like?

Plains

If you took a bike trip in the Southeast, you would have lots of flat plains to ride on. The plains near the Atlantic Ocean are called the Coastal Plain because they are near the coast. They have good soil and lots of water.

➤ **Put your pencil on the plains at the upper right part of this map. Trace a bike route as far south as you can. Make an <u>X</u> where you stop.**

Find the Savannah River. Suppose you decide to ride northwest along the river. Look at the map key. Would riding your bike get harder or easier? Why? Write your answer here.

_____

_____

The Southeast Region: Physical Map

Ohio R.
ALLEGHENY MTNS.
James R.
Roanoke R.
Cape Hatteras
OZARK PLATEAU
Tennessee R.
APPALACHIAN MTNS.
PIEDMONT
Mississippi R.
Red R.
Lake Pontchartrain
Alabama R.
Savannah R.
COASTAL PLAIN
Cape Fear
ATLANTIC OCEAN
C O A S T A L   P L A I N
Mississippi Delta
Gulf of Mexico
Cape Canaveral
N
W   E
S
Lake Okeechobee

KEY
▨ Mountains
⋰ Highlands
— Plateaus
☐ Plains

0   100 miles
0   150 kilometers

The Everglades
Florida Keys

Trees, vines, and flowers grow on the wet land of a swamp.

There are **swamps** in some parts of the Coastal Plain. A swamp is a place where the land is always wet. The **X** you made on the map on page 44 is near the Everglades swamp. Many plants and animals live in swamps. Alligators are one kind of animal that lives in the Everglades.

Look at the map and map key on page 44. Find the mountains. They are called the Appalachian Mountains.

➤ **Now look at the western part of the map. What is the longest river you see? Write your answer here.**

_____

The Mississippi River runs through the western plains of the region. It is the second-longest river in the United States. This river begins far north, in Minnesota. It travels south 2,340 miles to the Gulf of Mexico. The Mississippi is so wide that big ships can travel on it. The ships carry oil, coal, cotton, and many other products.

The Mississippi River is so full of soil that it looks like mud. Rains add water to the river. When the river has too much water in it, some spills out onto the land. Water that rises and covers the land is called a **flood**.

Floods can hurt people and damage their homes. But Mississippi floods also do some good. They leave **fertile** soil on fields. Fertile soil is land that is good for growing crops.

Barges carry goods on the Mississippi River.

Chapter Checkup ✓

➤ **Darken the circle by the answer that best completes each sentence.**

1. A gulf is like
- Ⓐ a bay.
- Ⓑ a river.
- Ⓒ a lake.
- Ⓓ an ocean.

2. Some hurricanes begin over the Gulf of Mexico or over the
- Ⓐ Mississippi River.
- Ⓑ Southeast.
- Ⓒ Northeast.
- Ⓓ Atlantic Ocean.

3. The Coastal Plain is flat and has lots of
- Ⓐ mountains.
- Ⓑ hurricanes.
- Ⓒ good soil.
- Ⓓ snow.

4. A swamp is
- Ⓐ dry.
- Ⓑ wet.
- Ⓒ snowy.
- Ⓓ very hot.

5. The second-longest river in the United States is the
- Ⓐ Everglades.
- Ⓑ Savannah.
- Ⓒ Mississippi.
- Ⓓ Ohio.

6. Water that rises and covers the land is a
- Ⓐ hurricane.
- Ⓑ gulf.
- Ⓒ swamp.
- Ⓓ flood.

Thinking & Writing

Why is the Mississippi River a resource for the Southeast Region? Give reasons for your answer.

_____

_____

_____

_____

_____

_____

46

People of the Southeast Region

CHAPTER 7

What is it like to live in the Southeast Region? Let's find out! First, we'll visit the region over 200 years ago.

Long Ago: Old Virginia in 1774

It's two o'clock and time for lunch. The King's Arms Tavern in Williamsburg, Virginia, is filled with people today.

The government of the colony meets here. Representatives from Virginia come to Williamsburg, the capital, to discuss laws.

➤ **Today, Williamsburg is not the capital of Virginia. Look at the map on page 42 and find the capital of Virginia. Write the name here.**

_____

King's Arm Tavern

The first governor wanted Williamsburg to become a big city. He made the streets straight, not like the curving streets in country towns. The main street of this city is 100 feet wide! Williamsburg has a school, but not everyone can go there. Most children have to help their parents in their shops. Slaves are not allowed to go to school. But there is a school for American Indians who want to learn to read and write English.

Williamsburg has lots of stores. Do you need a new pair of shoes? You can't just walk into a shoe store and buy them. First, the shoemaker has to measure your feet. Then, he'll make shoes to fit you. You can come back in a week to pick them up.

Blacksmith

There are many businesses here in Williamsburg. There's a blacksmith who works with iron and steel. He makes shoes for horses and fixes tools. And there are shops where barrels or baskets or wigs are made. People in Williamsburg wear wigs whenever they get dressed up.

That's how it was in 1774. If you visit Williamsburg today, you'll have a surprise. It never became a big city. In fact, it still looks the same! The King's Arms still serves meals, and people still make baskets by hand. That is because the city is a "living museum" where we can go to see how Americans lived here more than 200 years ago.

➤ **Write the name of a building in your town that you think should always be kept the way it is now. Tell why. Write your answer here.**

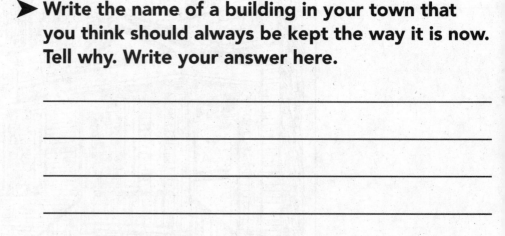

Many people enjoy the sun and sand at Miami Beach, Florida.

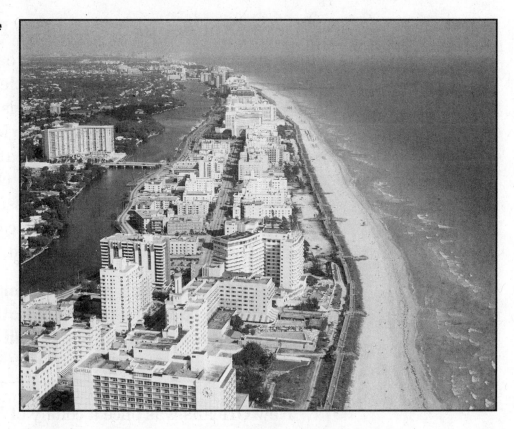

Who Lives in the Southeast Today?

Over 70 million people live in the Southeast. More than 60 million live in the Northeast. But the Southeast is not as crowded.

➤ **Compare the maps on page 28 and page 42. Which region has more land? Write your answer here.**

_____

Every year, more people move to the Southeast. Some people come to find jobs. Others come because they like warm weather. The lower part of the region is called the **Sunbelt** because it has a sunny climate.

People have moved to the Southeast from many parts of the world. From the 1600s to the early 1900s, many people came from Europe. Since the 1960s, thousands of people from Cuba have moved to Florida. People from China, the Philippines, and Vietnam have come to the region, too. Almost half of all African Americans in the United States live in the Southeast.

Where Do People Live in the Region?

In the Southeast, more people live in small towns than in cities. But there are large cities in each state of the region. New Orleans, Louisiana, is the busiest port city in the United States. It is on the Mississippi River.

Products and crops from many states are shipped to New Orleans on the river. At New Orleans, they are put on bigger ships. From the Mississippi River, the ships move out into the Gulf of Mexico. From the Gulf of Mexico, they can go around the world.

➤ **Look at the map on page 44. Ships leave the Gulf of Mexico to take products to other countries. If they go east, on what ocean will they travel?**

_____

New Orleans was once a colony of France. Later, France sold New Orleans to the United States. Some of the buildings in New Orleans look like old buildings in France. Other parts look very modern. In 2005, much of New Orleans was flooded by hurricane Katrina. The city is slowly recovering from great destruction.

Many tourists like to visit the French Quarter in New Orleans.

Atlanta, Georgia

Atlanta, Georgia, is one of the biggest cities in the Southeast. Atlanta was a small city until about 100 years ago. Everything changed when the railroads reached the city. First, the railroad companies built the rail lines along the Coastal Plain.

➤ **Why would railroad companies first build lines on the plain? Write your answer here.**

_____

_____

_____

Then, other railroads were built from the coast to the mountains. Atlanta was at the place where all the railroads met. So Atlanta became a good place to have a business. You could ship products from Atlanta all over the United States. Today, Atlanta is one of the most important U.S. cities for business. The 1996 Summer Olympic Games were held in Atlanta.

Miami, Florida, is very warm in the winter. People from the north like to take vacations there. Tourism is an important business in Florida all year long.

Working in the Southeast Region

The most important resource in the Southeast has always been fertile land. In the 1800s, cotton was the most important crop in the Southeast. People grew cotton on large farms called **plantations** and sold it to countries all over the world.

Cotton is still an important crop because we use it to make clothing. Factories in North Carolina make more cloth than factories in any other state in the United States. The flowchart on this page shows how cotton from the Southeast is used to make bluejeans.

➤ Write **SEW** on the picture that shows how pieces of cloth are put together with a sewing machine.

Write **SHIP** on the picture that shows how the jeans get to the stores.

How Bluejeans Are Made

Cotton is picked.

Cotton is made into thread.

Thread is dyed blue.

Pieces are sewn together.

Front, backs, and pockets are cut.

Thread is made into cloth.

Jeans are pressed.

Jeans are put into boxes.

Jeans are sent to stores.

The warm climate of the Southeast is good for growing certain crops. Most of the oranges grown in the United States come from Florida. Rice is another crop grown in the Southeast. Another important crop of the Southeast is peanuts. Did you know that peanut soup and peanut pie are popular foods in parts of the Southeast?

One city in the Southeast is known for a very different kind of product. Nashville, Tennessee, is called the capital of country music. Stars of country music make records there. The music business is one of the biggest businesses in the city.

Many people in the Southeast have service jobs. People all over the Southeast work in hotels, restaurants, stores, movie theaters, and in many other places where they help other people.

Cotton plant   Peanuts

➤ **List three important crops of the Southeast. Write your answer here.**

_____

Chapter Checkup ✔

➤ Darken the circle by the answer that best completes each sentence.

1. The city that still looks the way it did about 200 years ago is
- Ⓐ Atlanta.
- Ⓑ New Orleans.
- Ⓒ Miami.
- Ⓓ Williamsburg.

2. The Mississippi River is important to the city of New Orleans because
- Ⓐ the city needs a lot of water.
- Ⓑ ships carry products on it.
- Ⓒ farmers like to swim in the river.
- Ⓓ it is next to Atlanta, Georgia.

3. The busiest port city in the United States is
- Ⓐ New Orleans.
- Ⓑ Miami.
- Ⓒ Atlanta.
- Ⓓ Williamsburg.

4. Atlanta became a big city after
- Ⓐ the French Quarter was built.
- Ⓑ the farmers left.
- Ⓒ railroads reached the city.
- Ⓓ plantations were started.

5. Long ago, the biggest crop in the Southeast was
- Ⓐ cotton.
- Ⓑ peanuts.
- Ⓒ oranges.
- Ⓓ rice.

6. The city of Nashville is known for its
- Ⓐ buildings.
- Ⓑ music.
- Ⓒ railroads.
- Ⓓ bluejeans.

Name a place you would like to visit that still looks the way it did 200 years ago. Give your reasons.

_____

_____

_____

_____

_____

Name _____   Date _____

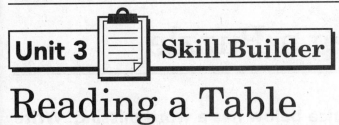

Unit 3 | Skill Builder

Reading a Table

You have read about some famous places in the Southeast Region. The table below tells you about more interesting places. Maybe you've already heard of some of them!

Famous Places in the Southeast Region

Place	Location	Description
Mammoth Cave	Kentucky	Unusual cave containing lakes, rivers, and waterfalls
Okefenokee Swamp	Georgia	Large swamp that is home to raccoons, opossums, alligators, bobcats, and many types of birds and plants
Walt Disney World	Florida	Huge amusement park visited by millions of people from around the world

➤ **Use the table to answer these questions.**

1. What state would you be in if you were visiting Okefenokee Swamp?

_____

2. If you visited Kentucky, what famous place could you visit?

_____

3. Which famous place would you visit if you wanted to see interesting animals?

_____

4. Which place was built by people?

_____

Unit 3 Activity

Working a Puzzle

➤ **Each sentence below has a word missing. Write the missing word in the correct location in the puzzle.**

ACROSS

2. A place where the land is always wet is called a _____.

4. A large body of water that joins an ocean and is partly surrounded by land is a _____.

6. The _____ River is wide enough for big ships.

8. The Southeast once had large farms called _____.

DOWN

1. A storm with strong winds and heavy rain is a _____.

3. The King's _____ was a tavern in Williamsburg.

5. New Orleans was once part of a colony belonging to _____.

7. Two important crops of the Southeast are cotton and _____.

Unit 3 ✏ Test

➤ **Darken the circle by the answer that best completes each sentence.**

1. The southern part of the Southeast Region is along the
   - Ⓐ Atlantic Ocean.
   - Ⓑ Gulf of Mexico.
   - Ⓒ Pacific Ocean.
   - Ⓓ Appalachian Mountains.

2. A large body of water partly surrounded by land is called a
   - Ⓐ lake.
   - Ⓑ port.
   - Ⓒ river.
   - Ⓓ gulf.

3. The Southeast sometimes has storms with strong winds and heavy rain called
   - Ⓐ gulfs.
   - Ⓑ swamps.
   - Ⓒ hurricanes.
   - Ⓓ floods.

4. The Mississippi River flows into the
   - Ⓐ Atlantic Ocean.
   - Ⓑ Pacific Ocean.
   - Ⓒ Everglades.
   - Ⓓ Gulf of Mexico.

5. Soil that is good for growing crops is
   - Ⓐ fertile.
   - Ⓑ muddy.
   - Ⓒ swampy.
   - Ⓓ in the mountains.

6. Two cities in the Southeast are
   - Ⓐ New Orleans and Atlanta.
   - Ⓑ New York and Chicago.
   - Ⓒ Philadelphia and Boston.
   - Ⓓ Baltimore and Cleveland.

7. The busiest port city in the United States is
   - Ⓐ Nashville.
   - Ⓑ New Orleans.
   - Ⓒ Miami.
   - Ⓓ Atlanta.

8. Two of the Southeast's important crops are
   - Ⓐ wheat and corn.
   - Ⓑ soybeans and rye.
   - Ⓒ peas and carrots.
   - Ⓓ rice and cotton.

Thinking & Writing

Why is the Mississippi River important to farming and manufacturing in the Southeast?

_____

_____

CHAPTER 8 Geography of the North Central Region

Like the Southeast Region, the North Central Region has 12 states. But the North Central Region is much flatter than the Southeast. There are few mountains and hills.

States, Cities, and Transportation

➤ **Suppose you have to drive to the 12 state capitals in the region. You can go into each state only once. Start in Columbus, Ohio. Use a pencil to draw lines to connect the 12 capitals on the map below.**

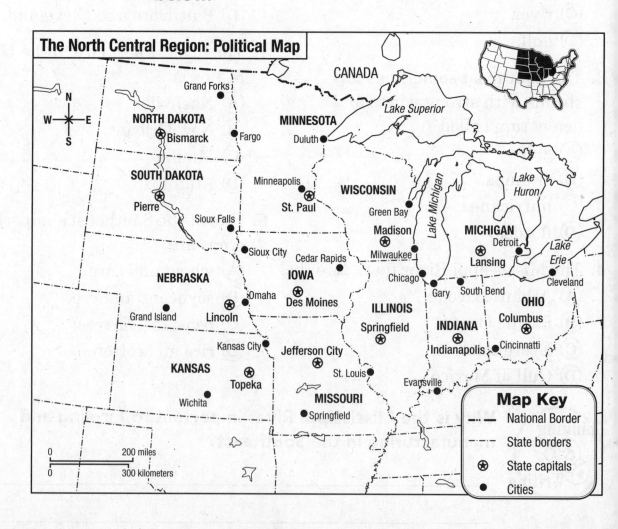

The North Central Region: Political Map

Map Key
- National Border
- State borders
- ⍟ State capitals
- ● Cities

The lines you drew on page 58 show a **route** of travel. A route is the way to go someplace. Look at the four maps on this page. Each map shows a different kind of transportation route. Airplanes fly between cities. Ships go on lakes and rivers. Cars and trucks drive on highways. Trains travel on railroads.

➤ **Look at the map called Main Air Routes. Each solid line shows an airplane route. Which city has the most airplanes flying in and out of it? Write your answer here.**

_____

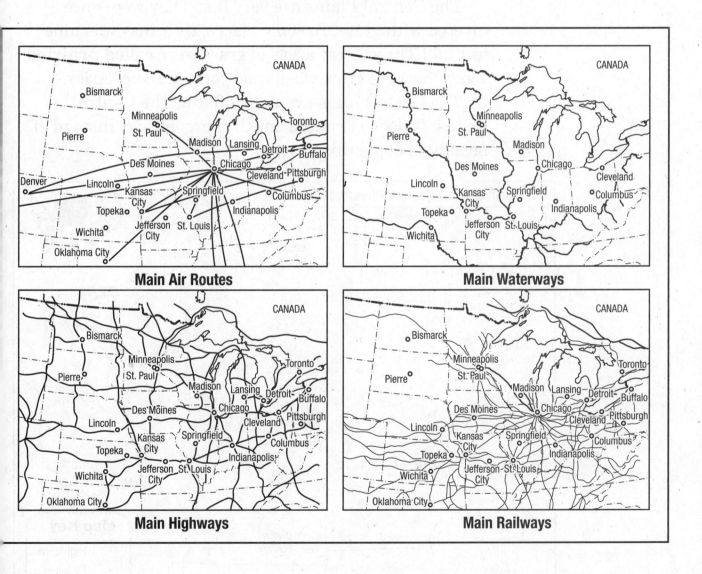

Main Air Routes

Main Waterways

Main Highways

Main Railways

The Land and the Great Lakes

When you studied physical maps of other regions, you learned that the key shows the shading that stands for different landforms.

Prairie

▶ **Look at the map and the key. Write the name of the landform that makes up most of the North Central Region.**

_____

▶ **Look at the west side of the map. Circle the words *Great Plains* and *Central Plains*.**

The Central Plains are very flat. They were once covered with grass. In some places, the grass was nine feet tall! These great areas of grass were called **prairies**. Today, farmers grow wheat and corn on the prairies.

The Great Plains are not as flat as the Central Plains. It doesn't rain as much there, either. Instead of farming, people raise cattle.

The North Central Region: Physical Map

Map Key
- Highlands
- Plateaus
- Plains

The North Central Region has lakes and rivers that ships can travel on. Some cities in the North Central Region are important ports.

➤ **Find the four biggest lakes on the map on page 60. Write their names here.**

_____

_____

We call these large lakes the Great Lakes. There is a fifth Great Lake, called Lake Ontario. It is in the Northeast Region. You can see Lake Ontario on the map on page 30.

Turn back to page 59. Look at the Main Waterways map. You can see that short rivers connect the Great Lakes. Longer rivers connect these lakes to cities and other rivers.

Look at the map on page 60. Find the dotted line that leads from Lake Michigan to the Illinois River. The dotted line is a **canal**. A canal is a waterway built by people. Canals link bodies of water so ships can travel from one waterway to another.

➤ **On the map on page 60, trace with a pencil the route a ship would take from Lake Michigan to the Mississippi River.**

There is much shipping on the Great Lakes.

Chapter Checkup ✓

➤ **Darken the circle by the answer that best completes each sentence.**

1. What is most of the land like in the North Central Region?
   Ⓐ hilly
   Ⓑ mostly rivers
   Ⓒ flat
   Ⓓ mostly plateaus

2. Which city has a very busy airport?
   Ⓐ Duluth
   Ⓑ Kansas City
   Ⓒ St. Louis
   Ⓓ Chicago

3. The two areas of plains in the North Central Region are the Great Plains and the
   Ⓐ Prairie Plains.
   Ⓑ Central Plains.
   Ⓒ Middle Plains.
   Ⓓ Northern Plains.

4. What is a prairie?
   Ⓐ a small mountain
   Ⓑ a great area of grass
   Ⓒ a large farm
   Ⓓ a lake

5. A waterway built by people is a
   Ⓐ canal.
   Ⓑ route.
   Ⓒ harbor.
   Ⓓ Great Lake.

6. Which of these is not a Great Lake?
   Ⓐ Superior
   Ⓑ Huron
   Ⓒ Minnesota
   Ⓓ Erie

Thinking & Writing

Airplanes travel faster than cars. Why might someone want to drive instead of fly?

_____

_____

_____

_____

_____

CHAPTER 9 People of the North Central Region

The pioneers headed west in covered wagons.

Many people went to the plains of the North Central Region in the 1800s. They were **pioneers**—people who go to live in a new place. Let's read a letter written in 1886 from Molly to her cousin Barbara. Molly writes about the trip her pioneer family took to the Great Plains.

Long Ago: The Treeless Plains

September 2, 1886
Dear Cousin Barbara,

You wanted to know how we are getting along since leaving Indiana. Well, I will tell you.

Two years ago, my mother and father decided to go to Nebraska, where there was a lot of free land. The government said anyone who would build a farm could have the land. This is called <u>homesteading</u>*. My parents thought that sounded like a pretty good deal.*

We left Indiana in a covered wagon. There is a railroad to Omaha, Nebraska, but tickets cost a lot of money. And my parents had to take along all their farm tools. We knew there weren't many stores in Nebraska.

➤ **Write the names of some things you think Molly's pioneer family needed.**

_____

_____

_____

The pioneers plowed fields and made butter.

We were very happy when we left for Nebraska. We sang songs all the way to the Mississippi River. There we met a man who said, "You're headed for the Great American Desert? Well, good luck, you'll need it."

He didn't mean the kind of desert that's full of sand. He meant that the land was flat and empty. Here in Nebraska there are no trees at all, just tall grass. And there aren't many rivers.

▶ **What landform is Molly talking about? Write your answer here.**

_____

When we reached our land in Nebraska, Father grabbed a shovel and started digging. "Look at this color," Father said. "This is the richest dirt I've ever seen. It will be easy to grow crops here."

Since there are no trees, my parents could not build the usual kind of house. Instead, they made one out of <u>sod</u>. Sod is blocks of dirt with grass growing in it. The roots of the grass hold the dirt together. My parents piled the blocks of sod on top of one another. Finally, we got our one-room sod house built.

It is dark inside our sod house. But it stays cool in the hot summers and warm in the cold winters.

I hope you and your family are well. Telling you about our life here in Nebraska has been fun. I hope you'll write again soon.

Love,

Cousin Molly

▶ **Look at the picture on this page. The pioneers are plowing fields and making butter. How do people do these things today? Write your answer here.**

_____

How Many People Live in the Region Today?

Over 70 million people live in the 12 states of the North Central Region. But more than half of these people live in just three states: Illinois, Ohio, and Michigan.

Why don't more people live in the other nine states? The main reason is that the nine states are where the farms are. Farms need lots of space.

Population is the number of people who live in a place. A population map gives you an idea of how many people live in an area. It also shows you where people live.

Find Nebraska on the map below. The dots and lines show where people live in that state. Notice that the dots are very far apart in some areas of the state. Those are farm areas. Now look at Ohio. The areas with many dots are near cities.

➤ **Which part of South Dakota has the most people?**

_____

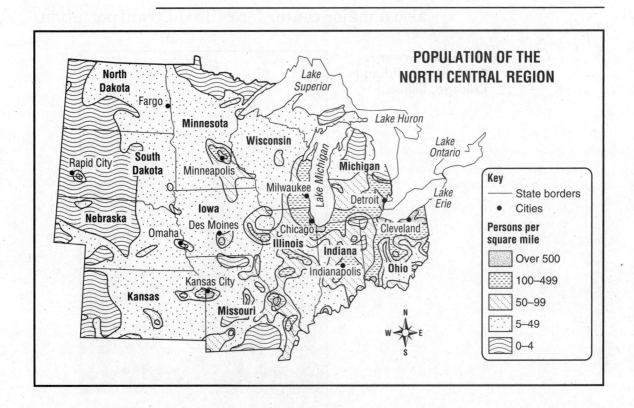

POPULATION OF THE NORTH CENTRAL REGION

Key
— State borders
• Cities

Persons per square mile
Over 500
100–499
50–99
5–49
0–4

Where Do People Live in the Region?

You know that most people in the region live in Illinois, Ohio, and Michigan. All of these states are near the Great Lakes. Many of the large cities of the region are ports on the Great Lakes. These cities have many factories and businesses. Let's take a look at some of these cities.

Chicago, Illinois, is the largest city in the region. It is the third-largest city in the United States. Almost three million people live there. Since the 1960s many immigrants from Mexico and Asia have moved to Chicago.

➤ **Find Chicago on the map on page 58. What Great Lake is it next to? Write your answer here.**

Chicago is a major transportation center. It is a major port. O'Hare Airport in Chicago is one of the largest and busiest airports in the world. Chicago is also a major center for railroad transportation.

The Sears Tower is the tallest building in Chicago, Illinois.

More than 80,000 people live in Duluth, Minnesota. Duluth is an important port city. Products like iron ore and grain are sent from Duluth to other places in huge ships. Some ships are as long as four city blocks!

➤ **One place the iron ore is shipped to is Gary, Indiana. Find Duluth and Gary on the map on page 58. What lakes would a ship travel across to get from Duluth to Gary? Draw the route you would follow on the map on page 58.**

St. Louis, Missouri, is a port on the Mississippi River. It began as a French colony. American Indians and other people took furs there to sell. People traveling west found it easy to get to St. Louis. Soon the city became a major port and a railroad center.

Today, all kinds of products are shipped from St. Louis. It is a bigger port than Chicago.

So many pioneers passed through St. Louis that it was called "the gateway to the West." The Gateway Arch celebrates that name.

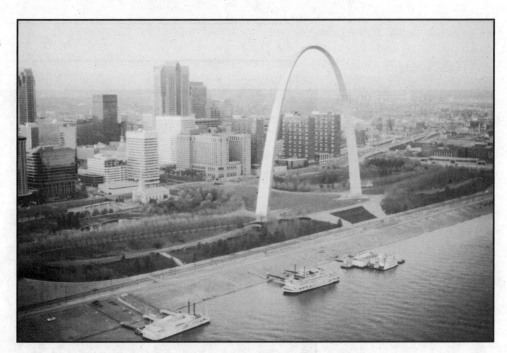

Working in the North Central Region

Service businesses are very important in the North Central Region. Other businesses are also important to the region. Near the Great Lakes, people manufacture a lot of things. On the plains, people have farms and ranches.

Many American cars are made near the Great Lakes. Detroit, Michigan, is the center of the United States automobile business. In 1903, Henry Ford began making cars in Detroit. His "Model T" was the first automobile that many people could buy.

The Model T was made on an **assembly line**. Each worker does one job over and over again on the cars on the assembly line.

➤ **Would you like to work on an assembly line? Why? Write your answer here.**

_____

_____

Cars are still built on an assembly line.

One of the reasons Henry Ford decided to build his factory in Detroit was because it is a port. Detroit is on a river between Lake Huron and Lake Erie. Ships carrying steel and other things used to build cars arrive in Detroit every day. Other ships carry finished cars from Detroit to other cities and to countries around the world.

Ships also travel across the Great Lakes carrying grains such as corn and wheat and other foods. Corn is the biggest crop grown in the North Central Region. Corn farmers of the region grow more corn than any other farmers in the world.

A lot of the grain grown in the region is fed to cattle and other animals. That's because there are many farms in the North Central Region that just raise animals.

➤ **What kind of land do a lot of ranchers use to raise animals in the region?**

_____

Dairy cattle are raised in every state of the region. We get milk, cheese, and other foods from dairy cattle. Part of your breakfast this morning may have come from a cow in Iowa!

The North Central Region is famous for its cheese and other dairy products. Here a worker tests some cheese.

Chapter Checkup ✓

➤ **Darken the circle by the answer that best completes each sentence.**

1. Under the homesteading plan, the government offered people moving to the Great Plains
   - Ⓐ a covered wagon.
   - Ⓑ land for farming.
   - Ⓒ five hundred dollars.
   - Ⓓ a brick house.

2. A sod house is made of
   - Ⓐ bricks.
   - Ⓑ wood.
   - Ⓒ rocks.
   - Ⓓ dirt.

3. The biggest cities in the North Central Region are near
   - Ⓐ lakes.
   - Ⓑ plateaus.
   - Ⓒ mountains.
   - Ⓓ oceans.

4. The city with the most people in the North Central Region is
   - Ⓐ Chicago, Illinois.
   - Ⓑ Detroit, Michigan.
   - Ⓒ St. Louis, Missouri.
   - Ⓓ Duluth, Minnesota.

5. The center of the American automobile business is
   - Ⓐ Duluth, Minnesota.
   - Ⓑ Chicago, Illinois.
   - Ⓒ Detroit, Michigan.
   - Ⓓ St. Louis, Missouri.

6. The biggest crop in the North Central Region is
   - Ⓐ cattle.
   - Ⓑ sugar.
   - Ⓒ milk.
   - Ⓓ corn.

Thinking & Writing

Write a menu for a meal that has at least two food items made from corn.

_____

_____

_____

_____

_____

_____

Unit 4 Skill Builder

Planning Routes

In this unit you learned that ships carry products from one Great Lakes port to another. But did you know that ships can travel from the Great Lakes all the way to the Atlantic Ocean? In the 1800s, people built canals to connect the Great Lakes to the St. Lawrence River, which flows into the Atlantic Ocean. Look at the map below.

1. Which Great Lake is connected to the St. Lawrence River?

_____

_____

2. Draw the route a ship would take to carry automobiles from Detroit, Michigan, to the port at Halifax, Nova Scotia.

3. Factories in Battle Creek, Michigan, need grain to make breakfast cereals. Ships carrying grain leave from Thunder Bay in Ontario, Canada. With your finger, trace a route from Thunder Bay to Detroit, Michigan. On which two Great Lakes will the ships travel?

Unit 4 Test

➤ **Darken the circle by the answer that best completes each sentence.**

1. The North Central Region has few
   - Ⓐ rivers and lakes.
   - Ⓑ large cities.
   - Ⓒ high mountains.
   - Ⓓ farms and factories.

2. A way to travel from one place to another is called a
   - Ⓐ route.
   - Ⓑ map.
   - Ⓒ distance scale.
   - Ⓓ prairie.

3. The five Great Lakes are Superior, Erie, Michigan, Huron, and
   - Ⓐ Illinois.
   - Ⓑ Atlantic.
   - Ⓒ Mississippi.
   - Ⓓ Ontario.

4. In the 1800s, the government gave land to people who agreed to build farms. These people were
   - Ⓐ Nebraskans.
   - Ⓑ American Indians.
   - Ⓒ homesteaders.
   - Ⓓ ranchers.

5. One way to connect two bodies of water is to build a
   - Ⓐ lake.
   - Ⓑ river.
   - Ⓒ harbor.
   - Ⓓ canal.

6. A map that shows about how many people live in an area is a
   - Ⓐ climate map.
   - Ⓑ population map.
   - Ⓒ weather map.
   - Ⓓ physical map.

7. Duluth, St. Louis, Detroit, and Chicago are
   - Ⓐ farming centers.
   - Ⓑ Great Lakes.
   - Ⓒ port cities.
   - Ⓓ capital cities.

8. Farmers in the North Central Region grow
   - Ⓐ rice and cotton.
   - Ⓑ wheat and corn.
   - Ⓒ prairie grasses.
   - Ⓓ sod.

Thinking & Writing

How would you choose to travel from Duluth to St. Louis—by car, by airplane, or by boat? Explain your answer.

_____

_____

Name _____   Date _____

CHAPTER 10 Geography of the Rocky Mountain Region

Where do you think the Rocky Mountain Region got its name? If you said from one of the region's major landforms, you're right. In this chapter, you'll find out about them.

Rocky Mountain States

➤ **Look at the map. The capital cities are far apart. Use the distance scale to measure the distance in miles between Helena, Montana, and Salt Lake City, Utah. Write the distance here.**

_____

Core Skills Social Studies 4, SV 9781419034268

The Rocky Mountain Region: Physical Map

CANADA

Missouri R.

Granite Peak

BITTERROOT RANGE

Salmon R.

R·O·C·K·Y

BIGHORN MTNS

Yellowstone R.

GREAT PLAINS

Missouri R.

N·M·O·U·N·T·A·I·N·S

Snake R.

N. Platte R.

Great Salt Lake

GREAT BASIN

Colorado R.

Mt. Elbert

Pikes Peak

Lake Powell

Lake Mead

0   100 miles
0   150 kilometers

Map Key

⧄ Mountains   — Plateaus

⋮ Highlands   ☐ Plains

······ Continental Divide

Mountains, Canyons, and Basins

The Rocky Mountains run through five of the six states of this region. The other state is on a high plateau. In Chapter 1 you learned that a plateau is a high, flat area of land.

➤ **Look at the map key on this page. Find the shading for plateaus. Which state is mostly a plateau? Write your answer here.**

_____

The Rocky Mountains are part of a long chain of mountains. This chain reaches from Alaska to the bottom of South America at the Andes Mountains. Look at the map on page 75. You can see where part of the Rocky Mountains stretches down from Canada and across the United States.

The Rocky Mountains are like the roof of a house. When rain falls on one side of a roof, it rolls off that side of the house. Look at the map on this page. The dark black line shows the **Continental Divide**. It is like the highest part of a roof.

➤ **Look at the "roof" next to the map below. Draw rain flowing down each side.**

All rivers that start to the west of the Continental Divide flow west, toward the Pacific Ocean. Rivers that start to the east of the Continental Divide flow east.

➤ **Find a river on the map that starts near the Continental Divide. Use a pencil to trace the river to an ocean.**

Look at the physical map on page 74. Find the high plateau to the west of the mountains. Write its name here.

Glaciers move at a rate of about a foot per day. As they move, they help to shape the land.

A **basin** is a landform shaped like a giant bowl. It has high sides all around. Once, the Great Basin was filled with water. There was a huge lake there. Over thousands of years, most of the water dried up. The water that is left now is so full of minerals, especially salt, that it is called the Great Salt Lake. Find the Great Salt Lake on the map on page 74.

It doesn't rain much in the Great Basin. Most of the water comes from ice and snow far up in the Rocky Mountains. Huge fields of ice and snow called **glaciers** lie on the highest slopes. Even in summer, the mountains are covered with snow.

As the snow melts, the water flows into rivers. The rushing waters pull away dirt and rocks, forming **canyons**. Canyons are deep, narrow valleys formed after hundreds of thousands of years.

➤ **Look at the photograph on the left. What natural resource made the canyon? Write your answer here.**

Moving water in rivers can carve away rock to form canyons.

Chapter Checkup ✓

➤ **Darken the circle by the answer that best completes each sentence.**

1. The Rocky Mountains run through all the states in the region except
   - Ⓐ Wyoming.
   - Ⓑ Idaho.
   - Ⓒ Nevada.
   - Ⓓ Colorado.

2. The Rocky Mountain chain stretches down from Alaska all the way through to the bottom of
   - Ⓐ Colorado.
   - Ⓑ South America.
   - Ⓒ Canada.
   - Ⓓ Nevada.

3. Rivers that are west of the Continental Divide flow toward the
   - Ⓐ Atlantic Ocean.
   - Ⓑ Pacific Ocean.
   - Ⓒ Great Basin.
   - Ⓓ Great Lakes.

4. A basin is a landform that is shaped like a giant
   - Ⓐ football.
   - Ⓑ castle.
   - Ⓒ bowl.
   - Ⓓ canyon.

5. The Great Salt Lake is located in
   - Ⓐ the Great Basin.
   - Ⓑ the Rocky Mountains.
   - Ⓒ the state of Colorado.
   - Ⓓ the Continental Divide.

6. Deep, narrow valleys are called
   - Ⓐ canyons.
   - Ⓑ basins.
   - Ⓒ mountains.
   - Ⓓ plains.

Thinking & Writing

Find Sparks, Nevada, on the map on page 73. Use what you learned in this chapter to describe what it might be like to live there.

_____

_____

_____

_____

CHAPTER 11 People of the Rocky Mountain Region

In this chapter you'll find out how people in the Rocky Mountain Region live today. But first let's meet one group who learned how to live in the region more than 150 years ago.

Long Ago in the Rockies: The Mountain Men

Jed Smith was born in New York State in 1799. As a boy, he learned how to live in the woods. At the age of 22, Jed headed west in search of adventure. He joined a group of explorers.

➤ **What do you think Jed Smith learned to do? Write your answer here.**

_____

A mountain man

Jed was very brave. Once, when he was in South Dakota, he was attacked by a very large bear. Jed was almost killed, but a month later he was strong enough to walk.

In the Rocky Mountains, Jed was a trapper. He caught animals and sold them for their fur. There were hundreds of men like Jed. They called themselves mountain men.

The mountain men had to spend a lot of time alone. They would hunt for 11 months. Then, in late summer, they would take the furs to a place where they could sell them.

The most important thing Jed owned was his gun. He used it to shoot animals for food. He also used it to keep large animals away. Next to his gun and his knife, a fur trapper like Jed needed his traps. He needed traps to catch beavers. He sold beaver furs to make a little bit of money.

Making money wasn't the most important thing to mountain men. Just staying alive in the wilderness wasn't easy. There were no doctors and no stores that sold food. Many mountain men learned the skills they needed to live in the Rocky Mountain Region from American Indians who lived there.

Most of the mountain men lived in the Rockies because they loved the mountains. They loved their free outdoor life.

By the early 1840s, the fur business was ending. Many mountain men built houses in the region. Others became guides for wagon trains bringing new **settlers** to the area. Settlers are people who go to live in a new part of a country. Today, there are no mountain men. They are part of the history of the Rocky Mountain Region.

► **Why do you think the mountain men were good guides for the new settlers?**

_____

Mountain men lived in the wilderness.

Some American Indian groups built their homes in canyon walls.

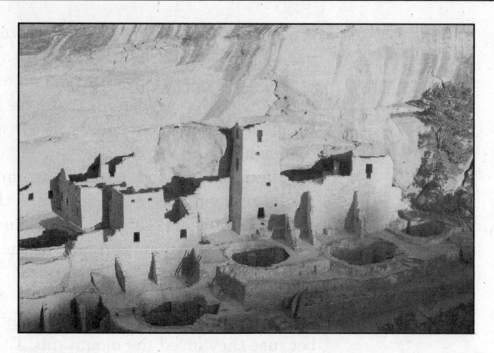

American Indians in the Region

The mountain men came to the Rocky Mountain Region in the 1820s. Small groups of American Indians had been living in the region for a long time.

During the 1800s, many new settlers came to the region. The American Indians and the settlers had different ideas about how to use the land. There were many battles. The United States government finally moved the Indians off the land and onto **reservations**. A reservation is land set aside by the government where American Indian groups can live. The reservations were often far from where the groups had been living. The land was not good for farming or hunting. Life on reservations was very hard.

Today, some American Indians still live on reservations in the Rocky Mountain Region and in other areas of the country. But American Indians do not have to live on reservations anymore. Like other citizens of the United States, they can live where they choose.

➤ **Why was life hard on the early reservations?**

Where Do People Live in the Region?

Today, more than 11 million people live in the Rocky Mountain Region. It has the smallest population of all the regions in the United States. As in other regions, most people in the Rocky Mountain Region live in cities. The city with the largest population is Denver, Colorado.

In the 1860s, Denver was a small town. People called **miners** were looking for gold and silver in the area. By the 1880s, a railroad had been built to Denver. More people and businesses moved there. Today, Denver is a major business and transportation center.

Denver is only ten miles from the Rockies. Temperatures are usually cooler up in the mountains than down on the plains. Look at the **line graph** below. A line graph shows how something changes over time. This line graph shows what the temperatures are like in Denver during the year.

Denver, Colorado, is known as the "Mile-High City."

➤ **What are the warmest and coldest months in Denver? Write your answer here.**

_____

MONTHLY NORMAL TEMPERATURE IN DENVER, COLORADO

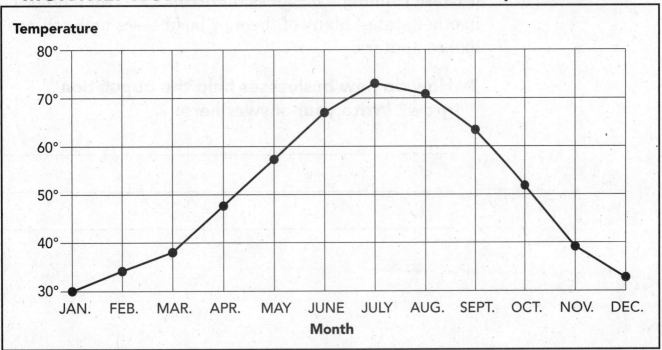

Another important city is near the Great Salt Lake. It is Salt Lake City.

➤ **Find Salt Lake City on the map on page 73. What state is it in? Write the state here.**

_____

Frontier Days Rodeo is a popular event in Cheyenne, Wyoming.

Salt Lake City was started in 1847 by a religious group called the **Mormons**. Like the Pilgrims, they wanted their own land and a place to worship. They worked hard and turned the dry lands into farms. Salt Lake City is still the center of the Mormon religion. More than two out of every three people who live in Utah are Mormons.

Cheyenne, Wyoming, has a population of about 53,000 people. Still, it is one of the biggest cities in the whole Rocky Mountain Region. Every year, people from all over the region visit Cheyenne. Many go to watch the Frontier Days **Rodeo**. A rodeo is a contest for cowboys and cowgirls. At rodeos they get a chance to show the skills they use in their jobs on cattle ranches.

Nevada has the fastest-growing population in the nation. Lots of new businesses have opened in Nevada because running a business there costs less than it does in other states. Many of the new businesses make things like computers.

➤ **How do new businesses help the population grow? Write your answer here.**

_____

_____

_____

Working in the Rocky Mountain Region

There are lots of ranches in the eastern part of the region. The Great Plains come right up to the mountains there. The land there is good for raising cattle.

➤ **Look at the maps on pages 73 and 74. What three states do you think are best for ranching? Write your answer here.**

_____

_____

People in the region also raise a lot of sheep. Sheep can live in the mountains, where the land is not good for farming or raising cattle.

People do some farming in the areas that are not in the mountains. Idaho is famous for growing potatoes. Idaho grows more potatoes than any other state! Farmers in Idaho and Montana also grow wheat and other grains.

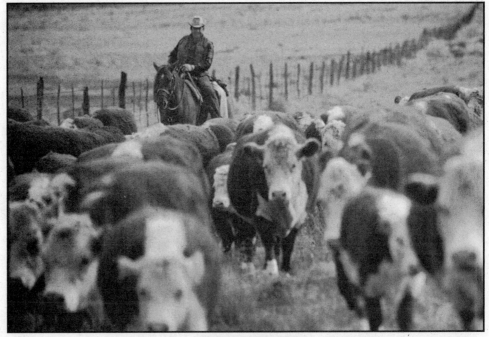

Raising cattle is an important business in the Rocky Mountain Region.

Mining is an important industry in this region. About 150 years ago, large amounts of minerals were discovered. Most of our gold and silver comes from this region.

Some of the mountains, lakes, rivers, and canyons are a resource because they are so beautiful. Each year millions of tourists visit the 11 national parks in the region. Park visitors can hike or simply enjoy the scenery.

Many people in the Rocky Mountain Region have tourism jobs. These include car rental agent, souvenir seller, and park ranger. These jobs are also service jobs. As in other regions of the country, there are more service jobs for people than any other kind of job.

➤ **What are three important jobs in the region? Write your answer here.**

_____

_____

Yellowstone National Park in Wyoming contains many natural wonders such as geysers and waterfalls.

Chapter Checkup ✓

➤ **Darken the circle by the answer that best completes each sentence.**

1. People who go to live in a new part of a country are called
   - Ⓐ guides.
   - Ⓑ mountain men.
   - Ⓒ settlers.
   - Ⓓ miners.

2. Of all the regions in the United States, the Rocky Mountain Region has the
   - Ⓐ most people.
   - Ⓑ fewest people.
   - Ⓒ best land for farming.
   - Ⓓ best land for houses.

3. Most people in the region live
   - Ⓐ in small towns.
   - Ⓑ in cities.
   - Ⓒ on farms.
   - Ⓓ on ranches.

4. In the 1800s, the United States government forced American Indians to move to
   - Ⓐ reservations.
   - Ⓑ cities.
   - Ⓒ farms.
   - Ⓓ national parks.

5. Salt Lake City was begun by a group of settlers called
   - Ⓐ American Indians.
   - Ⓑ cowboys.
   - Ⓒ mountain men.
   - Ⓓ Mormons.

6. Many people in the region have
   - Ⓐ tourism jobs.
   - Ⓑ teaching jobs.
   - Ⓒ fishing jobs.
   - Ⓓ shipbuilding jobs.

Thinking & Writing

Why do so few people live in the Rocky Mountain Region?

_____

_____

_____

_____

_____

_____

Unit 5 | **Skill Builder**

Reading a Line Graph

Large numbers of settlers first began coming to Nevada in 1859 when silver was discovered there. This line graph shows how Nevada's population has grown.

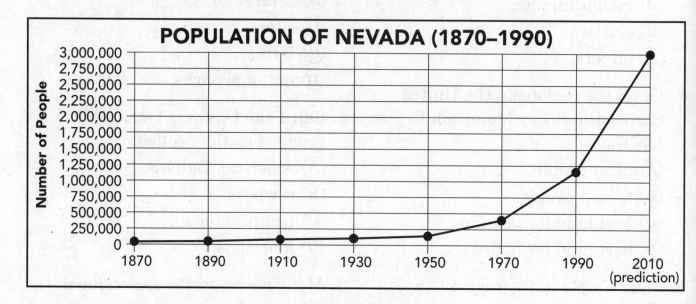

POPULATION OF NEVADA (1870–1990)

1. Circle the answer that tells what happened to Nevada's population between 1870 and 1990.

   It got bigger.   It stayed the same.   It got smaller.

2. When was Nevada's population about 200,000?

   _____

3. What was the population of Nevada in 1990?

   _____

4. Did the population grow more between 1930 and 1950 or between 1970 and 1990?

   _____

5. How would a line graph look for a town whose population got smaller?

   _____

Unit 5 Test

➤ **Darken the circle by the answer that best completes each sentence.**

1. The Rocky Mountain Region is mostly
   (A) flat.
   (B) mountains and plateaus.
   (C) plains.
   (D) sunny.

2. Two Rocky Mountain states are
   (A) Wyoming and Utah.
   (B) North and South Dakota.
   (C) Kansas and Arizona.
   (D) Cheyenne and Billings.

3. The Great Salt Lake is what is left of
   (A) a large river.
   (B) a huge lake.
   (C) a glacier.
   (D) the Pacific Ocean.

4. A deep narrow valley formed by rushing water is called
   (A) a basin.
   (B) the Continental Divide.
   (C) a canyon.
   (D) the highlands.

5. The Andes Mountains in South America are part of the
   (A) Appalachian Mountains.
   (B) Great Basin.
   (C) Rocky Mountain chain.
   (D) Great Plains.

6. Lands set aside by the government where American Indians can live are called
   (A) reservations.
   (B) farms.
   (C) ranches.
   (D) settlements.

7. The Rocky Mountain Region has many
   (A) cattle ranches.
   (B) pig farms.
   (C) cornfields.
   (D) chicken farms.

8. Important minerals mined in the Rocky Mountain Region are
   (A) coal and oil.
   (B) salt and sand.
   (C) iron and steel.
   (D) silver and gold.

What kinds of skills did the mountain men need to have?

_____

_____

Geography of the Southwest Region

CHAPTER 12

In the last unit, you read about a region that is full of mountains. The Southwest Region has mountains, too, but more than half of the Southwest is flat plains.

States and Cities of the Southwest

There are only four states in the Southwest Region. One of them is the second-biggest state in our nation. Can you find this state on the map below?

➤ **Draw a line from the state capital farthest west to the state capital farthest south.**

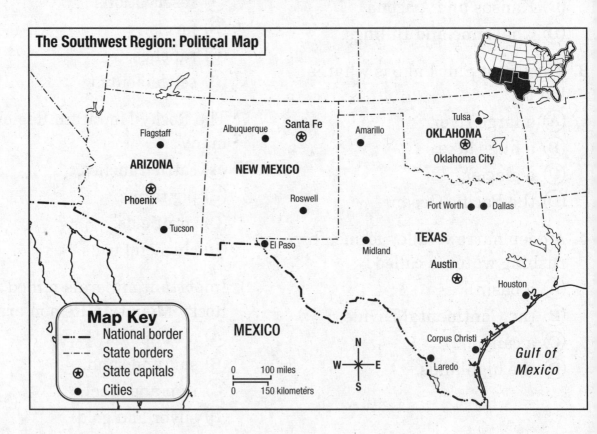

The Southwest Region: Political Map

Land, Rivers, and Climate

The land of the Southwest looks like a set of stairs. The lowest step is the Coastal Plain. Look at the map below. Find the words *Coastal Plain* near the Gulf of Mexico.

The Great Plains are the middle step. They are higher than the Coastal Plains but lower than highlands or mountains.

➤ **Arizona and New Mexico are the top step. Look at the map. What landforms make up these states? Write your answer here.**

_____

There are many rivers on the plains of Texas. There is only one major river in the highlands and plateaus of Arizona. It is the Colorado River. A long time ago, the Colorado River carved out the Grand Canyon. The Grand Canyon is a mile deep!

➤ **Find the Grand Canyon and the Colorado River on the map. Circle the Grand Canyon.**

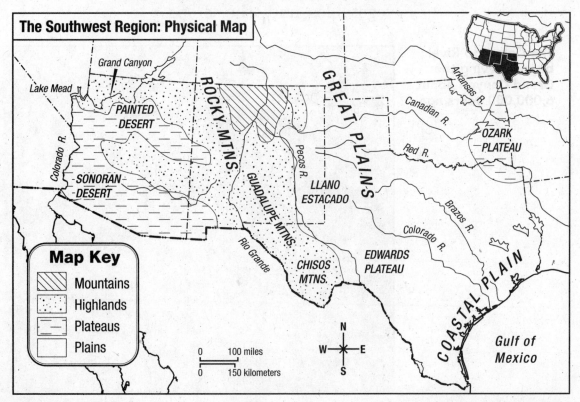

The Southwest Region: Physical Map

Grand Canyon

Lake Mead

PAINTED DESERT

ROCKY MTNS.

GREAT PLAINS

Arkansas R.

Canadian R.

OZARK PLATEAU

Red R.

Colorado R.

SONORAN DESERT

GUADALUPE MTNS.

Pecos R.

LLANO ESTACADO

Brazos R.

Rio Grande

CHISOS MTNS.

EDWARDS PLATEAU

Colorado R.

COASTAL PLAIN

Gulf of Mexico

Map Key
- ▨ Mountains
- ⦂ Highlands
- ▦ Plateaus
- □ Plains

0   100 miles
0   150 kilometers

N W E S

Parts of the Southwest are known for being hot and sunny. The Southwest is part of the Sunbelt. But this does not mean that the whole region has the same climate. On a day when oranges are growing in the south of Texas, it may be snowing in the north of Texas. Texas is a big state!

➤ **Turn back to the climate map on page 11. Find Texas. How many climate areas does it have? Write your answer here.**

_____

There are **deserts** in the Southwest. Deserts are dry lands with very little rainfall. Deserts in the Southwest can get very hot.

Desert plants have long roots that reach deep into the ground where there is water. Desert animals hide from the strong sun. They look for food and water at night.

People have found ways to bring water from far away to the desert. Watering crops by bringing water to an area where it is in short supply is called **irrigation**. With the help of irrigation, farmers can grow cotton, vegetables, and other crops.

The Colorado River began carving the Grand Canyon about 6,000,000 years ago.

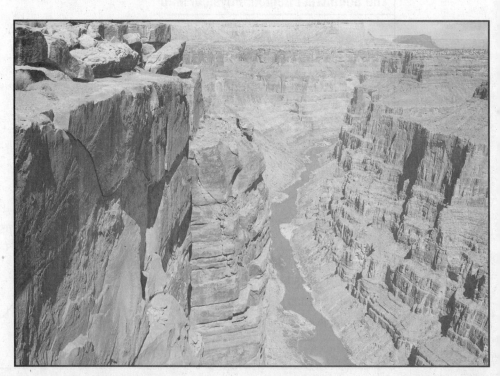

Chapter Checkup ✔

➤ **Darken the circle by the answer that best completes each sentence.**

1. More than half of the land in the Southwest is
   (A) mountains.
   (B) plateaus.
   (C) flat plains.
   (D) highlands.

2. The largest state in the Southwest is
   (A) Arizona.
   (B) New Mexico.
   (C) Oklahoma.
   (D) Texas.

3. Most of the rivers in the Southwest are in the
   (A) mountains.
   (B) plains.
   (C) deserts.
   (D) highlands.

4. The Grand Canyon was carved by
   (A) the Colorado River.
   (B) the desert.
   (C) American Indians.
   (D) irrigation.

5. Deserts are lands that have very little
   (A) warm air.
   (B) mountains.
   (C) rainfall.
   (D) sunshine.

6. When farmers bring water to dry land from far away, it is called
   (A) a coastal plain.
   (B) irrigation.
   (C) farming.
   (D) a desert.

Thinking & Writing

Would you rather visit the Grand Canyon or the desert? Give your reasons.

_____

_____

_____

_____

_____

_____

People of the Southwest Region

CHAPTER 13

American Indians were the first to live in the Southwest.

Many people settled in the Southwest in the past. Today, many people are still moving there. But who were the very first people to live in the region? American Indian groups arrived thousands of years ago.

Long Ago: The Comanche

The Comanche once ruled the plains. They were great hunters and fighters. They lived in small groups. They moved to find food. In summer they followed the herds of deer and buffalo across the plains. They dried some of the meat to eat during the winter.

For hundreds of years, Comanche children learned the same lessons. Fathers taught sons to hunt. Mothers taught daughters to prepare food and clothing from buffalo and deer.

➤ **Why do you think the Comanche dried meat for the winter? Write your answer here.**

_____

Then, about 300 years ago, a great change began. Other people arrived from Spain. They were ranchers who came to raise cattle. They brought horses with them to the Southwest.

Once the Comanche had horses, their way of life changed. They became great riders. It was easier to follow and hunt the buffalo herds.

Horses also made the Comanche strong in war. On horseback they were able to win more battles. By 1800, they ruled a large part of the Southwest.

Soon thousands of settlers moved to Texas. They moved there because they wanted to build farms and ranches.

The Comanche tried to make the settlers leave. Then United States soldiers attacked Comanche camps. The fighting went on for a long time. But the guns and soldiers did not beat the Comanche.

The Comanche were beaten by sickness. The settlers brought sicknesses from Europe. The Comanche had never had these sicknesses before. Thousands died. In the early 1800s, there were 30,000 Comanche. Fifty years later there were only half as many.

► **About how many Comanche were there in 1850? Write your answer here.**

_____

The Comanche were also beaten by the buffalo hunters with guns. The hunters killed the animals that the Comanche needed for food and clothing. These hunters killed as many buffalo as they could. In just a few years, the great buffalo herds were gone.

In 1875, the last Comanche were moved to a reservation. They were no longer allowed to move across the plains.

► **What two "enemies" hurt the Comanche most? Write your answer here.**

The Comanche needed the buffalo for food and clothing.

_____

Who Are the People of the Region?

Over 31 million people live in the four southwestern states. There are more American Indians and Mexican Americans in the Southwest Region than in any other region.

American Indian groups arrived in the Southwest long ago. The Navajo and Pueblo were living in the Southwest by the year 1300.

➤ **What groups of people lived in the Southwest Region about 700 years ago? Write your answer here.**

_____

During the early 1800s, most of what is now Oklahoma was known as Indian Territory. The United States government had set aside this land for American Indians. Many American Indians from different parts of the country had been forced to settle in Indian Territory.

By the 1880s, many settlers had come and set up cattle ranches all around Indian Territory. The settlers told the government they wanted the land in Indian Territory. The government told the American Indians they could sell the land. Many American Indians sold their land in Oklahoma.

In 1889, the government held a Land Rush—a race to claim land that had once been Indian Territory. Over 50,000 settlers entered Oklahoma in one day to get the land.

Today, a large number of American Indians live in the Southwest. Many live on reservations in the region. The Navajo reservation covers parts of Arizona, New Mexico, and Utah. It is the largest American Indian reservation in the United States.

The Oklahoma Land Rush

An adobe house in Santa Fe, New Mexico

People from Spain arrived in the Southwest in the 1500s. They built a colony in New Mexico in 1598, more than 20 years before the Pilgrims landed in the Northeast.

Spanish-speaking people have lived in the Southwest for hundreds of years. Until about 150 years ago, most of the Southwest was part of Mexico or a colony of Spain. All through the 1900s, thousands of Mexicans moved to the Southwest. Today, Mexican Americans make up one fourth of the population of the Southwest.

➤ **Look at the time line at the bottom of the page. A time line is a line that shows a number of years. Marks on the line stand for events that happened during those years.**

Some events of the Southwest Region are shown on the time line. This time line covers 700 years. Each small part of the time line stands for 100 years.

Write _1889_ where it belongs on the time line. Draw a line to the words that go with it.

How many years passed between the time when the first Spanish colony was started and the Land Rush? Write your answer here.

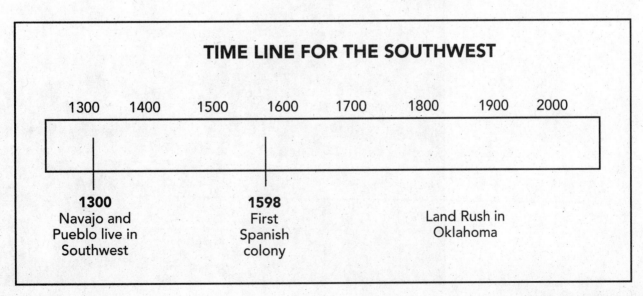

TIME LINE FOR THE SOUTHWEST

1300   1400   1500   1600   1700   1800   1900   2000

1300
Navajo and
Pueblo live in
Southwest

1598
First
Spanish
colony

Land Rush in
Oklahoma

Where Do People Live in the Region?

You have learned that there are deserts in the Southwest. There is not much water in the desert. Most people in the Southwest live in cities.

The city of San Antonio is by a river on the Texas plains. It began as a farming village. Because the weather is so warm there, farmers grow crops all year round.

Houston, Texas, is on several bayous. A **bayou** is a creek or small river. Buffalo Bayou was dug out to form the Houston Ship Channel. Houston became a major port after oil was discovered in Texas.

Oil is very important to many of the cities in the Southwest. Tulsa, Oklahoma, was an American Indian farming village. After oil was discovered there, it became a big business center. Now more than 350 oil companies have their offices there.

➤ **What business is important to both Texas and Oklahoma? Write your answer here.**

_____

Houston, Texas, is located on several bayous.

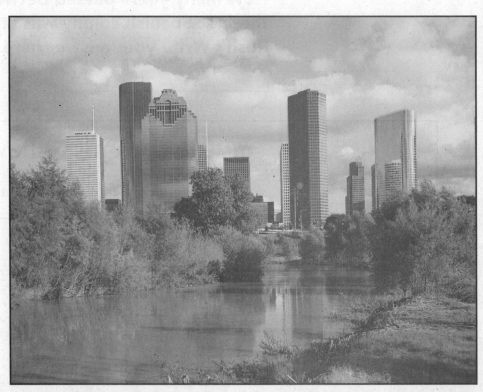

Some southwestern cities were built near old roads or trails. Many of these had been used by travelers for centuries. The city of Albuquerque started along a road. Later a railroad was built across New Mexico. Now Albuquerque is the largest city in the state.

➤ **How do you think the railroad helped Albuquerque grow? Write your answer here.**

_____

_____

Oklahoma City was one of the first towns settled during the Land Rush of 1889. Oil was discovered under the city in 1928. The city grew quickly after that.

Many cities in the Southwest have Spanish names. That is usually because they were started by the early Spanish settlers. Some houses in southwestern cities look like houses in Mexico. People often eat Mexican food and play Mexican music. The Southwest also has the largest Mexican American population in the country.

An American Indian girl in traditional dress

Traveling in the Southwest Region

How do drivers find the way to places they have never been before? Most of the time, they use road maps. Some maps also show places of special interest to travelers.

For example, pretend you're traveling through Oklahoma. You would like to find a campground where you can spend the night.

➤ **Look at the road map below. It shows part of Oklahoma. Look at the map key. Find the symbol for campground. Circle the campground you would reach by traveling on Interstate Highway 40.**

Now pretend you are traveling from the town of Chandler to the town of Goldsby. Find the town of Chandler in the northeast corner of the road map. Next, find the town of Goldsby. Now trace the roads you would follow to drive from Chandler to Goldsby.

Working in the Southwest Region

Ranching was the first business in the Southwest. People from Spain had started raising cattle in Texas by the 1700s. Ranching became more important as the United States grew. One Texas ranch grew bigger than the state of Rhode Island!

There were no railroads in Texas in the mid-1800s. So ranchers had to walk the cattle north to cities where there were railroads. These cattle drives were hundreds of miles long and very dangerous.

In the late 1800s, railroads were built to Texas. The long cattle drives were over. But cattle ranching is still an important business in Texas today.

➤ **Why do you think railroads ended the need for the cattle drives? Write your answer here.**

_____

_____

A cattle drive

Oil pumps are a common sight in Texas and Oklahoma.

Around 1900 a new business grew up in the Southwest—oil. The states of Texas and Oklahoma produce a lot of oil. Oil is used to make gasoline and other products. Cars, planes, and ships need gas and oil to be able to move. Homes and buildings are heated with oil. Plastics and many other products are made from oil.

Usually, oil is found far under the ground. Special wells are needed to pump it out. Then it must go to a place called a **refinery**. In a refinery, the oil is cleaned and made into different products.

Today there are many jobs in the oil business. What jobs will the Southwest have in the future? New jobs usually come from **research**. *Research* means "studying things and finding out about them." Research is often done by businesses and universities. Research scientists often solve problems by finding better ways to do things. For example, we know we have to be careful with our natural resources.

One thing researchers in the Southwest work on is new ways to use less oil. They study other types of energy that can be used. Have you ever heard of **solar energy**? Solar energy uses the heat of the sun instead of oil to heat homes.

➤ **If you did research, what would you want to study? Write your answer here.**

_____

Many people in the Southwest have service jobs. Like other regions of the United States, the Southwest needs teachers, doctors, salespeople, and other service workers.

Chapter Checkup ✓

➤ Darken the circle by the answer that best completes each sentence.

1. The first people to live in the Southwest were
(A) Spaniards.
(B) American Indians.
(C) settlers.
(D) Mexican Americans.

2. The Comanche were able to hunt better when they got
(A) sick.
(B) reservations.
(C) settlers.
(D) horses.

3. The largest American Indian reservation in the United States is that of the
(A) Comanche.
(B) Pueblo.
(C) Sioux.
(D) Navajo.

4. To get their cattle to market, ranchers had cattle drives to get to
(A) Texas.
(B) railroads.
(C) Mexico.
(D) rivers.

5. The states of Texas and Oklahoma produce a lot of
(A) soil.
(B) steel.
(C) electricity.
(D) oil.

6. One thing research scientists do is
(A) look for gold.
(B) move to Oklahoma.
(C) find better ways to do things.
(D) go on cattle drives.

Thinking & Writing

What job in the Southwest Region sounds the most interesting to you? Explain why.

_____

_____

_____

_____

_____

Unit 6 | Skill Builder

Reading a Road Map

Look at the road map of part of New Mexico. There is often more than one road you can take to the same place. Road maps can show you the shortest way.

1. What two kinds of roads appear on the map?

_____

2. Which federal highway goes through the Mescalero Apache Indian Reservation?

_____

3. What road would you take to travel from Roswell to Caprock? What direction would you travel?

_____

4. Someone tells you about the interesting caves at Carlsbad Caverns National Park. List the highways you would take from Caprock to Carlsbad Caverns.

_____

Unit 6 Test

➤ **Darken the circle by the answer that best completes each sentence.**

1. Two states in the Southwest are
   A Colorado and Kansas.
   B Nevada and California.
   C Texas and Oklahoma.
   D Arkansas and Louisiana.

2. The southern part of the Southwest Region is next to
   A Canada.
   B Mexico.
   C California.
   D Texas.

3. The Southwest has both mountains and
   A flat plains.
   B an ocean coast.
   C salt lakes.
   D large islands.

4. Lands that get very little rain are called
   A deserts.
   B highlands.
   C plains.
   D canyons.

5. Farmers in the Southwest bring water to their fields using
   A glaciers.
   B solar energy.
   C labor unions.
   D irrigation.

6. The people who have lived in the Southwest the longest are
   A American Indians.
   B pioneers.
   C from Spain.
   D immigrants.

7. Tulsa, Oklahoma, became a big business center after the discovery of
   A gold.
   B silver.
   C solar energy.
   D oil.

8. Long cattle drives ended when people built
   A ships.
   B refineries.
   C railroads.
   D reservations.

Which would be a better place to start a cattle ranch: the mountains of Colorado or the plains of Texas? Explain your choice.

CHAPTER 14 Geography of the Pacific Region

The Pacific Region is the only region where two of the states are separated from the rest of the United States. That is why its geography is the most varied and unusual of any region.

The West Coast States

Three of the Pacific Region states are called the West Coast states. Find them on the left map. Trace the edges of the three states with a pencil or crayon.

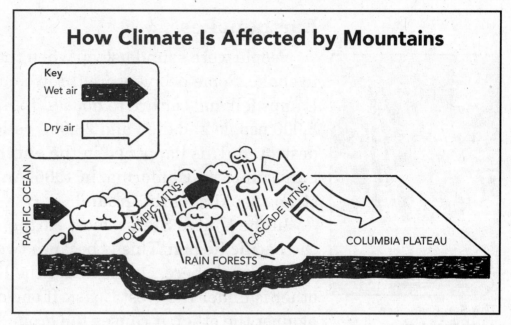

How Climate Is Affected by Mountains

All three states have mild climates. This is because the Pacific Ocean carries warm water and warm breezes from the south. They help keep the temperatures mild. They also cause more rain to fall in Oregon and Washington.

A **diagram** shows how something is made or how something works. Look at the diagram on this page. This diagram shows how climate is affected by mountains. The black arrows stand for wet air from the ocean. The wet air moves up the mountains. As the air moves higher, the temperature gets colder. The cold makes the wet air turn into rain. The rain falls on the west side of the mountains. By the time the air has crossed the mountains, it is much drier. Follow the arrows with your finger.

▶ **What do the white arrows on the diagram stand for? Write your answer here.**

_____

Look at the diagram again. The words on the diagram tell you about the land. Circle the words that tell you an area is very rainy.

Earthquakes

The San Francisco earthquake of 1906 caused great destruction.

People were sound asleep when the ground began to shake. Some people were thrown out of their beds! Lamps fell and set fire to houses. In a few hours, 3,000 people had died and 28,000 buildings had been destroyed. This happened in the **earthquake** that hit San Francisco, California, in 1906. An earthquake is a strong shaking of the ground.

In the United States, most earthquakes happen in the Pacific Region. This is because two gigantic areas of land meet there. One is under the Pacific Ocean. The other is under the West Coast. If one of them moves against the other, it causes the ground nearby to shake. The place where the two land areas meet is called a **fault**.

Most earthquakes in the Pacific Region are very small. The strongest earthquake in North America took place in Alaska in 1964. Scientists have equipment to measure how strong earthquakes are. They use a special scale called a Richter scale to measure the earthquake. The highest Richter scale ever measured was 8.9. The 1906 San Francisco earthquake measured 8.3.

▶ **What is an earthquake? Write your answer here.**

Seismographs measure and record Earth's vibrations.

Alaska: Political Map

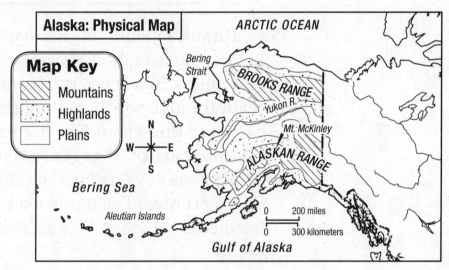

Alaska: Physical Map

Alaska

Alaska is the largest state in the United States. To reach Alaska from the state of Washington, you have to travel hundreds of miles north through Canada.

➤ **Look at the political map. Find the capital of Alaska and circle its name.**

Now look at the relief map. Find the plains in northern Alaska. This land is **tundra**—land that is too cold for trees to grow. Tundra soil is almost always frozen. Not all of Alaska is tundra. It is warm enough in southern Alaska for farmers to grow oats, barley, and potatoes.

Hawaii

Hawaii is farther west and farther south than any other state. It is hundreds of miles out in the Pacific Ocean. Hawaii is known for its mild, pleasant climate. Look at the top map. Find the islands of Hawaii.

➤ **Look at the physical map of the islands of Hawaii. Compare it to the physical map of Alaska on page 107. How are the two states alike? Write your answer here.**

_____

Hawaii's mountains are not like regular mountains. In fact, the islands of Hawaii were formed long ago by **volcanoes**. Volcanoes are openings in the crust of the earth through which melting rock, dust, ash, and hot gases are thrown up. The hot rock is called **lava**. When volcanoes **erupt**, they shoot lava into the air.

Millions of years ago, volcanoes under the Pacific Ocean erupted. The hardened lava formed the Hawaiian Islands. Even today, Hawaii's volcanoes erupt from time to time.

Hawaii has several active volcanoes.

Earth spins on an imaginary axis. The North and South poles are the two ends of the axis.

Dividing Earth

The Pacific Region states are spread over a large part of Earth. Look at the top globe on this page. Find the islands of Hawaii on the northern and western side of the globe. How do we know where north or west is? Earth looks like a big ball, and a ball does not have a top or bottom. Look at the first globe again. Earth turns on an imaginary **axis**, or center line. The axis goes from the North Pole to the South Pole.

We divide Earth into a northern half and a southern half. These halves are called **hemispheres**. The imaginary line where the two halves meet is called the **equator**. The globe in the middle shows the two hemispheres.

If we could cut Earth into a northern half and a southern half, it would look like this.

► **Put an <u>N</u> on the Northern Hemisphere and an <u>S</u> on the Southern Hemisphere.**

We also divide Earth into an Eastern Hemisphere and a Western Hemisphere. The imaginary line between these hemispheres is called the **prime meridian**. The line goes through the two big oceans. The bottom globe shows the prime meridian.

► **Put an <u>E</u> on the Eastern Hemisphere and a <u>W</u> on the Western Hemisphere.**

What two lines divide Earth into hemispheres? Write your answers here.

_____

_____

If we could cut Earth into an eastern half and a western half, it would look like this.

Chapter Checkup ✔

➤ **Darken the circle by the answer that best completes each sentence.**

1. The West Coast states of the Pacific Region are
   Ⓐ California, Oregon, and Alaska.
   Ⓑ California, Oregon, and Washington.
   Ⓒ Oregon, Hawaii, and Alaska.
   Ⓓ Washington, Oregon, and Alaska.

2. Warm Pacific Ocean breezes help make the climate of the West Coast states
   Ⓐ cold.
   Ⓑ hot.
   Ⓒ dry.
   Ⓓ mild.

3. As wet air gets colder, it produces
   Ⓐ deserts.
   Ⓑ rain.
   Ⓒ sunshine.
   Ⓓ warm air.

4. The land in Alaska that is too cold to grow trees is called
   Ⓐ Canada.
   Ⓑ snow.
   Ⓒ tundra.
   Ⓓ a volcano.

5. The islands of Hawaii were formed by
   Ⓐ earthquakes.
   Ⓑ tourists.
   Ⓒ volcanoes.
   Ⓓ tundras.

6. The northern and southern halves of Earth are called the
   Ⓐ prime meridian.
   Ⓑ fault.
   Ⓒ hemispheres.
   Ⓓ axis.

Thinking & Writing

Suppose you were going to move to Alaska or Hawaii. Which state would you choose? Explain your answer.

_____

_____

_____

_____

People of the Pacific Region

Panning for gold

Gold was discovered in California in 1848. People hurried there from all over. Here is a diary a gold hunter might have written.

Long Ago: The Gold Rush

20 October 1849   We finally got here, but it took us nearly four months. It was hard crossing the Rocky Mountains in a covered wagon. Our camp is called Rich Gulch. Many people are here already.

25 October 1849   My brother Jim and I got some land of our own. One man at Yuba River got 30 pounds of gold from his piece of land. So far we have only found a few dollars worth of gold. Everything costs a lot here.

24 November 1849   Most gold here is dust or tiny flakes. To find it, you put a handful of sand in a wash pan. Then you scoop up lots of water and move the pan in a circle to keep the sand moving. Gold is heavier, so it goes to the bottom. It is very hard work, and we are not finding much gold.

2 February 1850   Today I came back from San Francisco with food and tools. Right away, people tried to buy them from me. People paid me in gold dust. I got more gold selling supplies than we found in the river in three months! Tomorrow we are going back to San Francisco to buy more supplies.

➤ **Why were so many people at Rich Gulch camp? Write your answer here.**

111

Who Are the People of the Pacific Region?

The Pacific Region has as great a mixture of people and ways of life as you can find anywhere in the United States. People have moved to the region from all over the world. Many American Indians, Hispanics, and Asian Americans live in the Pacific Region.

American Indians came to the West Coast area thousands of years ago. Then Spanish colonists and Mexican Americans moved there. During the 1800s, pioneers from the East began moving to the West. At that time the West was known as the **frontier**. A frontier is the farthest edge of a country, where few settlers live.

Most pioneers headed for California or Oregon. Pioneers gathered at Independence, Missouri, where trails to the California, Oregon, and Washington regions began. Back then, the trails were really only tracks in the ground made by covered wagons that had traveled the trail earlier. The trip from Independence to Oregon on the Oregon Trail took six months! Large "trains" of covered wagons made the hard trip across deep rivers, deserts, and the Rocky Mountains. Often, the travelers ran out of food and water and got sick. Even though the trip was dangerous, by 1890 so much of the West had become settled that the United States government announced that the West was no longer a frontier.

▶ **Why do you think pioneers wanted to make the hard journey to the West Coast?**

_____

_____

Pioneers traveled by covered wagon.

This picture shows how the Tlingit of Alaska lived long ago. Their large plank houses provided shelter for many related families.

Many groups of American Indians, such as the Modoc and Yakima, lived near the West Coast. Before the settlers came, the American Indian groups fished, hunted, and used the trees of the forests to build boats and houses. The American Indians of the Pacific Region had many natural resources they could use.

When settlers and miners arrived, things changed. The settlers and the American Indians fought about how to use the land. Later, the government forced American Indian groups to go to reservations.

The Modoc was one group that fought against having to move to a reservation. But the government moved the Modoc to a reservation in Oregon. A chief named Kintpuash led a group of 80 families back to their old hunting grounds in California. The army tried to force them back to the reservation. For five long months, a small group of Modoc fought the soldiers. The Modoc finally lost the battle. They were moved to a reservation in Oklahoma.

The Yakima and many other Pacific Region American Indian groups still live in the West Coast states. Other American Indian groups such as the Inuit, Aleut, and Tlingit live in Alaska.

➤ **Why do you think the Modoc went back to California? Write your answer here.**

_____

_____

_____

_____

_____

_____

_____

Cable cars are a popular attraction in San Francisco, California.

Remember that during the 1800s most immigrants to the eastern part of the United States came from countries in Europe. Immigrants from Europe came to the West, too. They hoped to find gold or good land there. But immigration was also different in the West Coast area. In the middle of the 1800s, news of gold in California reached China. China is a country in Asia, which is across the Pacific Ocean. Immigrants from China came to California to look for gold. Because so many settlers were going west, railroad companies wanted to build railroads that would stretch all the way from the East Coast to the West Coast. Thousands of Chinese immigrants helped build the railroads.

▶ **Look at the time line below. What was the first West Coast state? Write your answer here.**

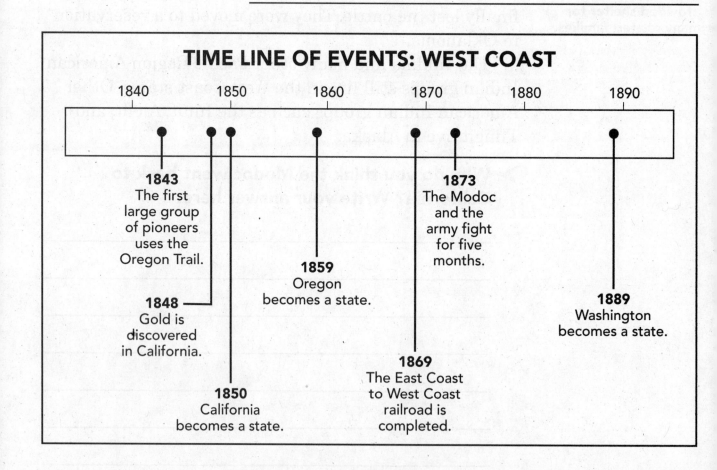

TIME LINE OF EVENTS: WEST COAST

| 1840 | 1850 | 1860 | 1870 | 1880 | 1890 |

1843
The first large group of pioneers uses the Oregon Trail.

1848
Gold is discovered in California.

1850
California becomes a state.

1859
Oregon becomes a state.

1869
The East Coast to West Coast railroad is completed.

1873
The Modoc and the army fight for five months.

1889
Washington becomes a state.

Where Do People Live in the Pacific Region?

About 45 million people live in the Pacific Region. Alaska is the largest state in the United States, but few people live there. California has the biggest population of all the states.

➤ **Why do you think Alaska has so few people?**

_____

Besides the Pacific Region states, there are hundreds of Pacific Islands in the region. The United States has been closely tied to many of these islands, offering them aid and protection. Some, like the Marshall Islands, have since become independent nations. Others, like Guam, the Northern Marianas, and American Samoa, are U.S. territories.

Honolulu is the largest city in Hawaii. It has one of the best harbors in the world. Because it is in the middle of the Pacific Ocean, Honolulu has become a busy and important port. In the past, ships going to and from Asia stopped there for fresh water and food.

Hawaii is a popular vacation spot.

The climate is very different in the states of the Pacific Region. Anchorage, Alaska, (left photo) is cold most of the year. Southern California (right photo) is warm all year round.

The city of Anchorage, Alaska, was once just a place where ships stopped. They were there to unload materials needed to build the Alaska Railroad. Today, Anchorage is the largest city in Alaska.

Two of the most important West Coast ports are Portland, Oregon, and Seattle, Washington. Neither one of these ports is near the ocean. Portland is 100 miles up the Columbia River. Ships go there to pick up lumber and other products. Seattle is 125 miles from the ocean. It is not on a river but on a large bay called Puget Sound.

Los Angeles, California, is the largest city in the Pacific Region. It is known for its busy highways, its beautiful beaches, and Hollywood, the movie capital of the world.

➤ **What are the names of three important ports in the Pacific Region? Write your answer here.**

_____

_____

Working in the Pacific Region

Look around your classroom. How many things do you see that are made of wood? Don't forget that paper is made from wood, too. The forests of Oregon and Washington provide many of the wood products we use.

The major product of Alaska is oil. The oil field in Alaska is bigger than any other in North America. A big pipeline carries the oil 800 miles from the northern part of Alaska to a harbor in southern Alaska. The pipeline is a very good way of transporting oil because roads cannot be built in the tundra areas of northern Alaska.

➤ **What do you think happens to the oil when it reaches the harbor? Write your answer here.**

_____

_____

_____

After trees are cut down, the logs are taken to lumber mills where they are cut into boards.

More than half of all the fruits and vegetables you eat are grown in the West Coast states. California and Washington are also important centers for technology. Many large computer and software businesses are located in these two states.

Since all the states of the Pacific Region are near the Pacific Ocean, you have probably guessed that fishing is important. Service jobs are also very important. Many people in the region have jobs related to the tourism business. The Pacific Region is an area of great beauty. Each year, millions of people from all over the world visit the mountains, volcanoes, lakes, rivers, and exciting cities of the region.

➤ **How is the Pacific Ocean a resource for the region?**

The giant redwood trees are a popular tourist attraction in California.

Chapter Checkup ✓

➤ **Darken the circle by the answer that best completes each sentence.**

1. In the middle 1800s, people rushed to California to find
   - Ⓐ trees.
   - Ⓑ houses.
   - Ⓒ gold.
   - Ⓓ fruit.

2. The farthest edge of a country where few settlers live is the
   - Ⓐ West Coast.
   - Ⓑ frontier.
   - Ⓒ Pacific region.
   - Ⓓ tundra.

3. Chinese immigrants helped build a
   - Ⓐ gold mine.
   - Ⓑ wagon trail.
   - Ⓒ pipeline for oil.
   - Ⓓ coast-to-coast railroad.

4. The largest city in Hawaii is
   - Ⓐ San Francisco.
   - Ⓑ Honolulu.
   - Ⓒ Hawaii City.
   - Ⓓ Anchorage.

5. Many of the Pacific Region's biggest cities are
   - Ⓐ important ports.
   - Ⓑ in the Central Valley.
   - Ⓒ not near water.
   - Ⓓ in Hawaii.

6. The largest oil field in North America is in
   - Ⓐ Texas.
   - Ⓑ Puget Sound.
   - Ⓒ California.
   - Ⓓ Alaska.

Thinking & Writing

Imagine it is 100 years ago. You are traveling from the East to the Pacific Region. Which state would you choose to settle in? Why? Write your answer here.

_____

_____

_____

_____

_____

Unit 7 | Skill Builder

Learning from a Diagram

What causes a volcano to erupt? Very deep down in the earth, there is melted rock called magma. During a volcanic eruption, the magma is pushed up through weaker rocks around it. When it reaches the surface of the earth, it is called lava. The diagram below shows you what a volcano would look like if it were cut in half.

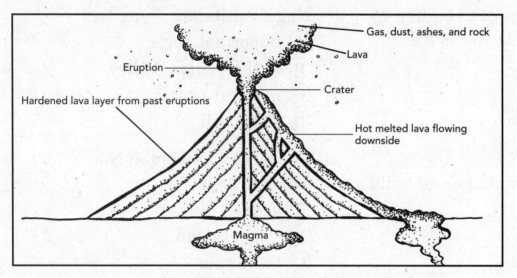

1. What is the bowl-shaped top of the volcano?

_____

2. What are the sides of the volcano made of?

_____

3. Trace one path of the magma to the surface.

4. Describe what you think it would be like to see a volcano erupt.

_____

Unit 7 Test

➤ **Darken the circle by the answer that best completes each sentence.**

1. The West Coast states of the Pacific Region are next to the
   - (A) Gulf of Mexico.
   - (B) Atlantic Ocean.
   - (C) Pacific Ocean.
   - (D) Puget Sound.

2. The mild climate along the West Coast is caused by
   - (A) ocean breezes.
   - (B) earthquakes.
   - (C) volcanoes.
   - (D) faults.

3. During an earthquake,
   - (A) there are strong winds.
   - (B) there is heavy rain.
   - (C) the ground shakes.
   - (D) the climate is mild.

4. Farmers in parts of Alaska grow
   - (A) oil.
   - (B) tundra.
   - (C) oats and barley.
   - (D) fruits and vegetables.

5. Hawaii was formed by
   - (A) earthquakes.
   - (B) people.
   - (C) islands.
   - (D) volcanoes.

6. In the 1850s, many people came to California to find
   - (A) oil.
   - (B) gold.
   - (C) deserts.
   - (D) volcanoes.

7. Oil is the most important product of
   - (A) Alaska.
   - (B) California.
   - (C) Hawaii.
   - (D) the West Coast states.

8. The Pacific Region raises most of the country's
   - (A) wheat.
   - (B) cattle and sheep.
   - (C) rice.
   - (D) fruits and vegetables.

How is the land of the Pacific Region different from the other regions you have studied?

_____

_____

east

north

south

west

Asia

Australia

Indian Ocean

Arctic Ocean

Europe

Africa

Antarctica

Atlantic Ocean

South America

North America

Pacific Ocean

THE WORLD

The United States

east

north

south

west

Atlantic Ocean

Pacific Ocean

New Hampshire
Vermont
Maine
Massachusetts
Rhode Island
Connecticut
New Jersey
Delaware
Maryland
New York
Pennsylvania
West Virginia
Virginia
North Carolina
South Carolina
Florida
Ohio
Kentucky
Tennessee
Georgia
Alabama
Michigan
Indiana
Illinois
Missouri
Arkansas
Mississippi
Louisiana
Wisconsin
Iowa
Minnesota
North Dakota
South Dakota
Nebraska
Kansas
Oklahoma
Texas
Montana
Wyoming
Colorado
New Mexico
Idaho
Utah
Arizona
Washington
Oregon
Nevada
California
Hawaii
Alaska

United States Map
Core Skills Social Studies 4, SV 9781419034268

Glossary

American Indian (page 13) An American Indian, or Native American, was one of the first people to live in America.

assembly line (page 68) On an assembly line, each worker does one job over and over again.

axis (page 109) Earth's axis is the imaginary line through the center of Earth from the North Pole to the South Pole.

basin (page 76) A basin is an area of land shaped like a bowl, with high sides all around.

bay (page 31) A bay is a body of water that is almost surrounded by land.

bayou (page 96) A bayou is a small river or large creek.

border (page 4) A border is an imaginary line between states or nations.

canal (page 61) A canal is a waterway built by people that links bodies of water.

canyon (page 76) A canyon is a deep, narrow valley.

capital (page 29) A capital is the city where government leaders meet.

climate (page 10) Climate is the kind of weather a place has over time.

climate map (page 10) A climate map shows the climate in different areas.

coast (page 8) A coast is the land that runs along the ocean.

colonist (page 14) A colonist is a person who lives in a colony.

colony (page 14) A colony is a land and people ruled by another country.

communicate (page 38) To communicate is to share information.

Congress (page 21) Congress is the group of people who make the nation's laws. The U.S. Congress is made up of the Senate and the House of Representatives.

continent (page 4) A continent is a large body of land.

Continental Divide (page 75) The Continental Divide is an imaginary line through the Rocky Mountains. Rivers that start to the west of the Continental Divide flow west. Rivers that start to the east of the Continental Divide flow east.

democracy (page 21) A democracy is a form of government in which the people have equal rights and choose their own leaders.

desert (page 90) A desert is an area of dry land that gets very little rainfall.

diagram (page 105) A diagram shows how something is made or how something works.

earthquake (page 106) An earthquake is a strong shaking of the ground.

equator (page 109) The equator is an imaginary line around the middle of Earth that divides Earth into a northern and a southern half.

erupt (page 108) To erupt is to shoot lava into the air, as a volcano does.

fault (page 106) A fault is a long, deep break in Earth's surface.

fertile (page 45) Fertile soil is land that is good for growing crops.

flood (page 45) A flood is water that rises and covers land that is usually dry.

frontier (page 112) A frontier is the farthest edge of a country, where few settlers live.

geography (page 4) Geography is the study of Earth and how we live on it.

glacier (page 76) A glacier is a huge field of ice and snow.

government (page 20) A government is a group of people who make the rules and lead others in towns, cities, states, and countries.

governor (page 21) A governor is a person who leads a state.

gulf (page 43) A gulf is a large body of water that lies along a coast and joins an ocean.

harbor (page 31) A harbor is an area of water that is protected by land from wind and strong waves.

hemisphere (page 109) A hemisphere is one half of Earth.

highland (page 30) A highland is hilly land between flat land and mountains.

homesteading (page 63) Homesteading is living and working on land given by the government.

House of Representatives (page 21) The House of Representatives is a part of Congress. The number of members depends on the population of their states.

hurricane (page 43) A hurricane is a storm with very strong winds and heavy rain.

immigrant (page 16) An immigrant is a person who leaves one country to live in another.

irrigation (page 90) Irrigation is watering crops by bringing water to an area where it is in short supply.

landform (page 8) A landform is a shape of the land, such as a mountain or hill.

lava (page 108) Lava is hot, melted rock from inside a volcano.

law (page 20) A law is a rule made by a government.

line graph (page 81) A line graph uses lines to show how something changes over time.

local government (page 20) A local government is a group of people who make the laws and lead the people of a town or city.

manufacturing (page 38) Manufacturing is making goods.

mayor (page 21) A mayor is a person who leads a town or city.

miner (page 81) A miner is a person who digs for minerals in the earth.

mineral (page 23) A mineral is something made by nature that is found in the earth. Silver is a mineral.

moisture (page 10) Moisture is how wet the air is.

Mormons (page 82) The Mormons are a religious group who went to Utah to find land and a place to worship.

Native American (page 13) A Native American is an American Indian, one of the first people to live in America.

natural resource (page 23) A natural resource is something from nature that people need and use.

physical map (page 8) A physical map gives information about types and shapes of land such as mountains and plains.

pioneer (page 63) A pioneer is a person who goes to live in a new place.

plain (page 8) A plain is a low, flat area of land.

plantation (page 51) A plantation is a very large farm.

plateau (page 8) A plateau is a high, flat area of land.

population (page 65) Population is the number of people who live in a place.

port (page 31) A port is a place where ships can load and unload goods.

prairie (page 60) A prairie is a large area of land with grass but few trees.

President (page 21) The President is the person who leads the United States.

prime meridian (page 109) The prime meridian is an imaginary line that runs north and south and divides Earth into an eastern and a western half.

recycle (page 23) To recycle is to reuse resources in order to keep from running out of those resources.

refinery (page 100) A refinery is a place where oil is cleaned and separated into different products.

region (page 6) A region is an area that land is divided into for study.

research (page 100) Research means studying things to find out about them.

reservation (page 80) A reservation is land set aside by the government where American Indian groups can live.

rodeo (page 82) A rodeo is a contest for cowboys and cowgirls.

route (page 59) A route is a way or plan of travel to take from one place to another.

Senate (page 21) The Senate is a part of Congress. There are two members from each state in the Senate.

service (page 20) A service is something that helps people.

service job (page 22) A service job is a job in which a person does something to help other people.

settler (page 79) A settler is a person who goes to live in a new part of a country.

slave (page 16) A slave is a person who is owned by another person.

sod (page 64) Sod is blocks of dirt with grass growing in it.

solar energy (page 100) Solar energy is the energy from the sun's heat.

state (page 4) A state is one of the 50 political units in the United States.

suburb (page 35) A suburb is a small town or city that is near a big city.

Sunbelt (page 49) The Sunbelt is part of the southern United States, where it is usually warm and sunny.

swamp (page 45) A swamp is an area of soft land that is always wet.

temperature (page 10) Temperature is how hot or cold the air is.

transportation (page 35) Transportation is how people or goods travel from one place to another.

tundra (page 107) A tundra is a cold, treeless area where the ground is almost always frozen.

united (page 4) United means together.

volcano (page 108) A volcano is an opening in the crust of the earth through which melting rock, dust, ash, and hot gases are thrown up.

vote (page 21) To vote is to make a choice.

weather (page 10) Weather is how hot or cold it is. Moisture is also part of weather.

Core Skills Social Studies 4, SV 9781419034268

Answer Key

NOTE: For answers not provided, check that students have given an appropriate response and/or followed the directions given.

Page 4
Students should write the letters *U.S.* next to the United States on the map on page 5. They should put a check mark on Mexico.

Page 5
north

Page 8
Students should identify the West as having more mountains. They should write an *X* in the coastal plain on the East Coast on the map on page 9, an *M* on the Appalachian Mountains, and a *P* on the plateau near the Arkansas River.

Page 9
Students should write an *M* on the Rocky Mountains.

Pacific Ocean

Page 10
temperature and moisture

Students should circle the Pacific coast on the map on page 11.

cool summers

Page 11
warm winters

Page 12
1. D   2. D   3. C   4. C   5. A   6. C

Answers will vary. Accept all reasonable answers.

Page 13
Asia

Page 14
1680: 150,000; 1740: 900,000

Page 15
American Indians helped the colonists by teaching them how to grow food.

American Indians and colonists had different ideas about the way the land should be used.

Page 16
Students should circle Germany.

Page 18
1. A   2. C   3. B   4. B   5. B   6. A

Answers will vary. Accept all reasonable answers.

Page 21
Students should circle President.

Page 22
Manufacturing

Page 24
Students should answer that we know we have to be careful about how we use natural resources so we will not run out of them.

Page 25
1. B   2. C   3. B   4. D   5. B   6. C

Answers will vary. Accept all reasonable answers.

Page 26
1. 1950–2002   2. Mexico   3. more than 500,000
4. Answers will vary. Accept all reasonable answers.

Page 27
1. A   2. C   3. D   4. C   5. B   6. C   7. A   8. D

Answers will vary. Accept all reasonable answers.

Page 28
Students should write an *N* on Maine and an *S* on Maryland.

Page 29
about 100 miles

Page 31
Students should write two of the following as their answers: Narragansett Bay, Delaware Bay, Chesapeake Bay, or Boston Bay.

Students should trace any two of these rivers: Kennebec, Connecticut, Hudson, Delaware, or Potomac.

Page 32
1. B   2. B   3. A   4. A   5. C   6. B

Answers will vary. Accept all reasonable answers.

Page 33
They wanted to practice their own religion.

Page 34
It was too cold and late in the season to plant crops, and many Pilgrims died.

The American Indians had lived there longer.

Page 35
400 miles

Page 36
Providence, Rhode Island; Dover, Delaware; Annapolis, Maryland.

Both groups of colonists left England to practice their religions.

Page 37
nine states

Firefighters put out fires and save people.

Page 39
1. B   2. D   3. B   4. C   5. A   6. D

Answers will vary. Accept all reasonable answers.

Page 40
1. about $1\frac{1}{2}$ miles   2. about $\frac{1}{2}$ km
3. about 3 km   4. $\frac{1}{2}$ mile

Page 41
1. C 2. B 3. C 4. D 5. A 6. C 7. B 8. C

Answers will vary. Accept all reasonable answers.

Page 42
Students should write an *N* on West Virginia and an *S* on Florida.

Page 43
Students should circle Virginia, North Carolina, South Carolina, Georgia, and Florida.

Hurricane Katrina in 2005 caused the most damage.

Page 44
Bike routes should begin at the top of Virginia and end with an *X* at the southern tip of Florida.

Bike riding would get harder because the plains would change to highlands and the highlands would change to mountains.

Page 45
Mississippi River

Page 46
1. A   2. D   3. C   4. B   5. C   6. D

Answers will vary. Accept all reasonable answers.

Page 47
Richmond, Virginia

Page 49
the Southeast

Page 50
the Atlantic Ocean

Page 51
It is easier to build a railroad on flat land.

Page 52
Students should write *SEW* on the sixth picture and *SHIP* on the ninth picture.

Page 53
Students should name three of these: cotton, peanuts, rice, oranges.

Page 54
1. D   2. B   3. A   4. C   5. A   6. B

Answers will vary. Accept all reasonable answers.

Page 55
1. Georgia   2. Mammoth Cave
3. Okefenokee Swamp   4. Walt Disney World

Page 56
1. hurricane 2. swamp   3. Arms 4. gulf
5. France   6. Mississippi 7. rice   8. plantations

Page 57
1. B 2. D 3. C 4. D 5. A 6. A 7. B 8. D

Answers will vary. Accept all reasonable answers.

Page 59
Chicago

Page 60
plains

Students should circle the words *Great Plains* and *Central Plains*.

Page 61
Students should answer Lake Superior, Lake Michigan, Lake Huron, and Lake Erie.

Students should trace a route from the southern tip of Lake Michigan, southwest along the dotted line to the Illinois River, down this river to the Mississippi.

Page 62
1. C   2. D   3. B   4. B   5. A   6. C

Answers will vary. Accept all reasonable answers.

Page 64
plains or Great Plains

People use machines today.

Page 65
the eastern part

Page 66
Lake Michigan

Page 67
Students should draw a shipping route through Lake Superior, into Lake Huron, and into Lake Michigan.

Page 69
plains

Page 70
1. B   2. D 3. A   4. A   5. C   6. D

Answers will vary. Accept all reasonable answers.

Page 71
1. Lake Ontario
2. Check students' routes.
3. Lake Superior and Lake Huron

Page 72
1. C 2. A 3. D 4. C 5. D 6. B 7. C 8. B

Answers will vary. Accept all reasonable answers.

Page 73
450 miles

Page 74
Nevada

Page 75
the Great Basin

Page 76
rushing water

Page 77
1. C   2. B   3. B   4. C   5. A   6. A
Answers will vary. Accept all reasonable answers.

Page 81
July and January

Page 82
Utah

New businesses create jobs, and people move to the places where there are jobs.

Page 83
Montana, Wyoming, and Colorado

Page 85
1. C   2. B   3. B   4. A   5. D   6. A
Answers will vary. Accept all reasonable answers.

Page 86
1. It got bigger.   2. 1950
3. 1,200,000   4. between 1970 and 1990
5. The line might start higher and go down instead of up.

Page 87
1. B   2. A   3. B   4. C   5. C   6. A   7. A   8. D
Answers will vary. Accept all reasonable answers.

Page 88
Students should draw a line from Phoenix, Arizona, east to Austin, Texas.

Page 89
plateaus, highlands, plains, and mountains

Page 90
three

Page 91
1. C   2. D   3. B   4. A   5. C   6. B
Answers will vary. Accept all reasonable answers.

Page 93
15,000

sickness and buffalo hunters

Page 94
the Navajo and the Pueblo

Page 95
291 years

Page 96
oil

Page 101
1. B   2. D   3. D   4. B   5. D   6. C
Answers will vary. Accept all reasonable answers.

Page 102
1. federal and state highways
2. Federal Highway 70
3. Federal Highway 380 east
4. west on 380, south on 285 to 62/180

Page 103
1. C   2. B   3. A   4. A   5. D   6. A   7. D   8. C
Answers will vary. Accept all reasonable answers.

Page 105
dry air

Students should circle the words *RAIN FORESTS* on the map.

Page 106
An earthquake is a strong shaking of the ground.

Page 107
Students should circle Juneau.

Page 108
Both Alaska and Hawaii have lots of mountains.

Page 109
the equator and the prime meridian

Page 110
1. B   2. D   3. B   4. C   5. C   6. C
Answers will vary. Accept all reasonable answers.

Page 111
They were all looking for gold.

Page 112
Answers might include to find a better life, to explore a new area, and to live in a less crowded place.

Page 114
California

Page 116
Answers may include Honolulu, Hawaii; Anchorage, Alaska; Portland, Oregon; Seattle, Washington; and Los Angeles, California.

Page 118
People catch fish from the ocean. The ocean and its beaches attract tourists.

Page 119
1. C   2. B   3. D   4. B   5. A   6. D
Answers will vary. Accept all reasonable answers.

Page 120
1. crater
2. hardened lava from past eruptions
3. Check students' tracings.
4. Answers will vary.

Page 121
1. C   2. A   3. C   4. C   5. D   6. B   7. A   8. D